HOW TO BECOME A COMPLETE ALCOHOLIC

How To Become A Complete Alcoholic

A satire by

Eric Burdick

NEW ENGLISH LIBRARY
TIMES MIRROR

First published in Great Britain by New English Library, 1974

•

FIRST NEL PAPERBACK EDITION DECEMBER 1975

•

NEL Books are published by
New English Library Limited from Barnard's Inn, Holborn, London, E.C.1.
Made and printed in Great Britain by Hunt Bar nard Printing Ltd., Aylesbury, Bucks.

45002553 5

THE ASMOLIAN EXPERIMENTS

being

The 1973 Asmolian Lectures
Given to the Staff and Students

at

The Asmolian Institute

by

Professor Asmol

Contents

An Asmolian is one whose altered metabolic and related psychic systems are such that the drug Alcohol ($C_2H_5.OH.$) is not the same drug as that consumed by the norm.

Professor Asmol

Asmolianism in the Modern Business World

My dear patients, staff, fellow colleagues, and to those who will be reading these lectures in book form, may I first of all admit to two 'irregularities' which will arise during my talks to you. One is the question of defining one's terms; the other is a matter of form.

To deal with the latter first: it is normal when developing a thesis, to start at some simple point of mutual agreement and from there, with inexorable logic, to progress to a comprehensive conclusion. This, as far as it is possible, I will attempt. But I must point out now, that so unusual, not to say revolutionary, is the Asmolian approach to alcohol that it cannot be separated from the work and achievements of the Asmolian Institute itself. And our experiments and our successes did not altogether follow a truly logical pattern. Sometimes a failure – and I would be the first to admit to a depressingly large number of these – forced us to retrace our steps and to start again at some point earlier on in our evolving system. At other times sheer luck, or purely accidental discoveries, would put us streets ahead in some sector of our learning. Thus it was, for example, that we stumbled across Korsakoff's Psychosis in our first experiment with a human subject. Now Korsakoff's Psychosis is, as you may know, symptomatic of an advanced stage of what is called alcoholism. Thus it really should be dealt with somewhere near the end of these lectures. However, as I have said, the Asmolian approach to alcohol is quite revolutionary and is thus open to all kinds of reactionary criticism. And I feel that the best, and perhaps the most honest, way to deal with criticism is to be as informative as possible about the beginnings and the developments of the Institute. Thus Korsakoff's Psychosis will, we trust, appear at the beginning of the lectures, just as it did with us at the Institute.

The other problem is, as I mentioned, the definition of terms. The reason I am going to define my terms as I go along – instead of getting it over with immediately – is simply because the study of alcohol is bedevilled, confused and in the end rendered totally negative by sloppy and widely differing terms of reference. In no other science – if indeed, work done before the founding of the Asmolian Institute can be called a science – has emotionalism, prejudice and downright amateurism led to such dismal lack of progress.

Therefore in my first lecture, I intend to deal with a far simpler question. *That is – why should one become an alcoholic?* Or more precisely (and already the problem of terminology is cropping up) why should one induce and develop the Asmolian Syndrome?

In answering this question I must first point out that there are people – not many, but some – who have so vegetated their minds and personalities, who have cemented so many prejudices into their thought patterns, that they find the Asmolian System, as a way of life, unacceptable. To these unfortunates, to these victims of our inhuman social myths and pressures, we can but extend our most profound (and admittedly useless) sympathy. To offer them Asmolianism is much the same as offering dinner at Maxim's to a marble statue. There's nothing wrong with the offer, but the recipient is dead.

Fortunately, however, almost anyone with a spark of humanity left in them can, by the use of Asmolian techniques, fan that spark to life's mightiest roaring bonfire and thus achieve, in whatever direction their individual make-up may take them, their ambitions, their hopes and even their most tortured fantasies. And having mentioned the word ambition I must point out that it is in this sphere, in the realm of worldly advancement and the acquisition of material success, that the Asmolian Syndrome proves to be nothing short of miraculously catalystic.

This is so for two reasons; one of which is obvious and the other of which was discovered only after lengthy and comprehensive social surveys made by the Institute.

The first reason is the simple fact that alcohol is an invigorating stimulant, a beneficial depressant to the central nervous system, a liberating elixir, a juice of the Gods and the Muses, a potion of creativity and the very foundation of inspired decisions.

The second reason was discovered, as I say, by a massive survey carried out by the Institute. What we wanted to know was this:

> What do the Top People in Great Britain, those who wield enormous power and guide the destiny of the nation, those who choose their colleagues and successors and who trample on both mediocrity and potential rivals – what do these individual giants, who collectively run the country, have in common?

Our survey showed – and in doing so vindicated my long held suspicion – that they had, almost to a man, developed a thoroughly robust Asmolian Syndrome. Or to put it in the sloppy and now totally outdated terminology of the medical profession – over eighty seven per cent of the nation's most powerful and influential people are advanced alcoholics.

From these facts we can immediately draw two conclusions.

> First: only alcohol can raise a person in stature and by achievement to a position where he will be considered, by those already in a position to do so, for admission to the upper echelons of riches and power.
>
> Secondly: those in this fraternity of might, like those in any cabal, can be expected to act and to decide in a truly tribal manner. They will accept those who share with them their most preponderant characteristic. Equally, they will reject and castigate (their motives being a combination of disgust, fear of implied criticism plus distrust of alien bodies) those who are not irrevocably committed to their scale of values.

All this can best be exemplified by a little story which I think should be told during my first talk to you. Let me say at once that this incident, which came to light through one of our patients, was of such interest to me that I had it followed up, investigated and recorded. Every person concerned has been interviewed by myself personally and I have not the slightest doubt that every detail is utterly factual. Needless to say, those of you who have advanced some way with the Asmolian Syndrome will recognise instantly the behavioural patterns, the symptoms, and in one case – most regrettably and, I assure you, quite inadvertently – the personal tragedy, as those of a classic alcoholic Asmolian situation.

*

Our story concerns the Managing Director and two senior executives of a major company involved in the manufacture and distribution of Industrial Hygiene and Sanitary Units. Our day begins at 8 a.m. in a highly respectable suburb of London. At that time Julius Clarron, one of the two senior executives, awoke.

Well, awoke is not quite the word. Let us say that at this time reality, as it is generally known, entered the life of Julius Clarron with a blinding, groaning confusion of vague and indescribable pain. Four hours previously Clarron had passed into oblivion with an alcoholic blood count far in excess of any machine designed to measure it. But in those four hours metabolism, oxidization and digestive consumption had taken their inevitable toll. During a full minute, reminiscent of the more harrowing scenes in the hunting of Moby Dick, he was pushed back into existence like a bottle of tomato ketchup going through a mincing machine. Blood seemed everywhere. His mind was a churning sea of broken glass and all around him the noise of total destruction bellowed in agonizing decibels.

At the end of the minute he realised that he was in fact Julius Clarron and that he was awake in bed. This necessitated a simple but highly important three point count-down. The first point of this count-down was to ascertain whether or not he was in his own bed. His eyes searched, as they had hundreds of times before, for the dark crack in the corner of the ceiling. *Yes, it was there*! And below it, the door with his dressing gown. Now for point number two.

With every limb in his body shaking like some weird death rattle he prised his pain-wracked, sweat-soaked, shivering body from the bed and trembled to the window. Moving the curtain to one side he peered out into the street to inspect the state of his car. In this he was not successful, for there appeared to be no sign of the car. Pulling the curtain fully open he stared fiercely at each car in front of the house. None was his. With hands shaking to such an extent that he seemed to be waving goodbye to the pedestrians outside, he gingerly opened the window, stuck his head out and scanned the entire length of the road. No car. Point number two was definitely negative.

The third point of his count-down was to find out whether his wife would speak to him. He turned from the window and made a statement in the direction of the bed.

' 'ood 'orning,' he said and immediate pain shot through the back of his head and shut his eyes to stop them from popping out, 'darling'. His wife turned in the bed and looked at him.

'God,' she said in a rather tired voice. 'I hope you feel as bad as you look.' As an after-thought she added: 'You drunken pig.'

Well, it wasn't good, but at least she was talking to him. Clarron reviewed his situation. Point one was positive. Point three was faulty but operational. Point two, however, was a sinister void – a black pit full of dangerous possibilities. He decided to make the tea.

In the kitchen, Susie, a medium sized white poodle, awoke as her master descended the stairs. A gentle, kindly-disposed dog at any other time of day, she was now simply an apprehensive canine as she awaited the arrival of Clarron. As soon as he opened the door she knew exactly his condition and what to expect. With a single whimper she slunk from her basket to the furthest corner of the kitchen.

'Bloody hound,' mumbled Clarron as he stood dazed in the middle of the cold room, looking for the kettle. This he filled with water and placed, rather loudly, on the cooker.

Julius Clarron then did something that can only be described as being suicidally motivated. He knew what he was doing. He knew well what the result would probably be. Nevertheless, he slowly and deliberately began to light a cigarette Susie whimpered in the corner.

'Shut up, you filthy cur,' snapped Clarron and aimed his bare foot.

The first puff wasn't too bad. Admittedly it was a small one and he didn't inhale too deeply. The second puff, rather larger and intended to be fully satisfying, proved to be his undoing.

He coughed. Just one cough, but he felt immediately that his stomach was cramping. Saliva seemed to fill his mouth and his brow was suddenly both hot and cold with sweat. He coughed again . . . then another . . . and another . . . and suddenly he was choking and wheezing and his stomach had gone into a bizarre spasm of pumping contraction. He stumbled to the sink and shouted something urgently important down the plug-hole. It sounded like: 'Aaaar, aaar, ahooh! aaaaaaa *gugglegoosh!*

The stream of fluid which issued from Mr Clarron's face was stringy in consistency and had a blueish-green colouring. It smelled of industrial acid, Spanish cooking – and discharged gunpowder. A second bout of 'aaar, aaar, ahooh! aaaaaaa *gugglegoosh*! produced a more solid substance with a distinctly yellowy colour. In fact, it was not unlike an omelette just before it sets.

The 'gawks' were nothing new to Clarron, but each attack seemed more vile, more painful and more degrading than any he had ever suffered. Now he stood huddled over the sink, yellow saliva drooling from his lips, sweat running down the side of his face and has entire body rattling epilectically. He turned on the cold tap and immersed his head under the tepid jet of water. He consoled himself with the fact that at least it was only a double attack of the gawks, not the dreaded triple ones, which, after an agony of honking, produce only small purple bubbles.

He turned from the sink and felt his way along one of the

lower shelves of the tall kitchen sideboard, searching for a towel.

It was then that Susie, contrary to all her Pavlovian learning, whimpered. Clarron opened his stinging eyes and saw Susie backed firmly into the corner. As he approached her she reared up on her hind legs, pressed herself even further into the corner – and snarled. With his eyes still blurred from the water Clarron let fly a mighty kick. He missed the dog and with a sickening crack his foot rammed into the Model One-Eleven Super-Silent Night Storage Block Heater.

Mr Clarron now performed an acrobatic feat of such dexterity that it would win him star billing in any of the world's larger touring circuses. He jumped in the air: having jumped with one foot, he precipitated himself to the left: while in the air he revolved ninety degrees. The result was that, at an altitude of one and a half feet, he crashed into the sideboard and, as ill-fortune would have it, grabbed the top shelf. With much creaking and clanking the already over-laden sideboard came away from the wall and, with Clarron hanging perilously from the shelf, the entire edifice crashed to the ground. The whistling kettle began to scream an insane banshee. Susie threw a fit of hysterical barking. And from somewhere under the sideboard, amid a shower of broken crockery, Mr Clarron moaned to his Maker.

*

At about the same time, Reginald Sard, the other senior executive in our story, was finishing a large and healthy breakfast. He had risen early, carried out his extensive Canadian Air Force exercises, bathed, shaved, dressed and read the morning post. Later he would take the train to work, delving deep into his brief case and organising his mind for the day's work ahead.

*

It was while Julius Clarron was waiting for a taxi, (he didn't really feel up to public transport) that the telephone rang sharply and painfully. Clarron's mind was suddenly filled with the fearful dread that it could be a Superintendent Inspector of Police at the other end. *Yes, they had traced the car's registration number. Very serious indeed. Mounted the pavement and killed two people. Tragic, really. Just a small girl pushing her crippled grandfather home in a wheel-chair. Anyway, it was a hit-and-run affair. Drove on till he crashed into an ambulance which was itself engaged in a critical maternity case. That was tragic too. The delay cost the lives of both mother and baby. He'd made a run for it.*

Clarron lifted the receiver.

'Yes, yes, yes,' he mumbled.

'Ah Jules,' came the thick voice of Sir Alexander Saunders. 'Thought you might already have left.'

In fact Julius' Managing Director sounded as if he were speaking through a wet towel.

'Great night, eh? Never knew you could do an Inca war dance. At least, not on the top of a table in the Club Fanfini.'

'Club Fanfini?' Julius queried meekly.

'Christ, you sound terrible. Thing is Jules, I've a spot of bother. Would you mind picking me up on the way in?'

'Funny you should ask that,' Julius began. 'Ah, . . . my car doesn't appear to be here at the moment. Taxi's on the way, though. Did we, ah . . . leave our cars somewhere? You know, safely parked? Some sensible place?'

'Not me, old boy. My car's here.'

'Is there something *wrong* with it, then?'

'Well,' Sir Alexander explained, 'I haven't inspected it too closely. Main problem is simply the fact that it's approximately four and a half feet through my garage door.'

'God.'

'And it occurs to me,' Saunders went on, 'that it didn't get there silently. Neighbours must have thought they were back in the days of the V2. Anyway, they can't see into my grounds and they probably don't know what the hell it was. But, Jules, to get the car out would no doubt be just as noisy and last a great deal longer. And heaven knows what state the car's in – though these Bentleys are supposed to stand up to some pretty vigorous driving.'

'Taxi's here,' Clarron announced nervously. 'I'll be with you shortly.'

When the taxi, after six life spans of aborted space travel, eventually arrived at the Saunders' demesne, Julius himself had difficulty recognising the ashen-faced individual who stumbled out of the massive front door – but a pale shadow of the well-known, robust and aggressive figure of Sir Alexander Saunders, voted last year's Man of Elan. But it was Saunders who spoke first as he opened the door of the taxi, apparently examining every detail of Clarron's face. 'God save us Jules, no wonder you can't find your car. You must have written it off against a glass factory. Have you had those lacerations seen to?'

'This,' and Clarron waved a feeble hand towards what remained of his physiognomy. 'This happened about an hour ago.'

'You look in pretty bad shape altogether.' Sir Alexander paused. 'Have you . . . you know . . . yet?'

Julius shook his head slowly in the negative. 'You?'

'No, no. But I think, under the circumstances . . . perhaps . . . Driver, wait on for a moment, will you?'

Saunders gingerly led the way across the ever-treacherous gravel, through the pressing gloom of the giant portcullis, along the frighteningly wide hall and into the comparative snug of his private – and somehow secret – study.

'I suppose at this time of the day it had better be the *Breathless Wonder*.'

'Sound,' agreed Clarron, and Sir Alexander Saunders, with groping paws, produced a bottle of Vodka.

'Care to pour?' Saunders asked.

'Dodgey,' Clarron replied.

'That bad, eh? Well, let's have a division of labour then. I'll attempt to pour if you reach in and get the glasses.'

With a fearful amount of clinking and clanking Julius manged to extricate two glasses. Saunders made a noble attempt at pouring and wiped the resulting mess off his desk with his clean handkerchief. The tonic fared little better, but eventually they each had a drink in their hands.

'No gawking now, Julius. Her Ladyship thinks I was at a

very staid meeting of the Institute of Directors.'

Julius took a sip, screwed up his face in pain – and swallowed. After a short gasp he asked:

'What about the car?'

'Stolen,' Saunders stated loudly after he too had dropped the first difficult gulp. 'Sheer vindictiveness. Thieves obviously thought it would be a great joke to drive it through my garage door.'

'Good,' Clarron nodded. 'Very good. What happened, anyway?'

'Damned if I know. I must have been doing forty up the drive. Lucky I didn't go through the window, but as far as I can see, not a bruise. And what about you?'

Saunders was again showing some interest in Clarron's shattered features. 'Go to bed with a gorilla?'

'No,' Clarron explained, taking a slow and shakey sip from his glass. 'We had a prospective new client get in touch with us. Very worried about the condition of one of our competitor's products – a supercharged waste-disposal unit. His worries were well founded. I, personally, for the safety of our men, went to dismantle the thing and it blew up on me.'

'Good,' Saunders nodded. 'Very good. What happened, anyway?'

'Bloody sideboard fell on top of me.'

'Extraordinary!' Saunders bellowed, quite out of context, taking the cork from the bottle. 'Let's have the other half then we'll go and look for your car.'

*

The first stop was to be the Club Fanfini. On the way, Saunders complained of the pressures at the top.

'And this maniac Gold! Why does our biggest client also have to be the biggest bastard imaginable? And why did I, in a fit of intoxication, undertake to handle the account myself? Now Gold's gone on the dry! Hasn't touched a drop in weeks.'

'With what result?'

'He's discovered his equipment isn't being serviced properly. Of course it isn't being serviced properly. For God's sake Jules, my job is to lay down general lines of policy, not running a maintenance department. So this morning I'll have to try to get *some*body to do *some*thing. And then this afternoon a Board Meeting. God, what insufferable hell.'

'With fifty-one percent of the stock, you're very worried?'

'Most of my co-directors,' Saunders replied testily, 'have the happy knack of being able to cure themselves at lunch. But I'm a five o'clock man myself. Which means, by four in the afternoon, they're all merry as hell and enjoying a great feeling of relief, while I have to sit there with the screaming horrors. And this afternoon's could prove particularly difficult. I suppose there's something on the grapevine about it?'

'Yes,' Clarron agreed. 'A new appointment to the Board.'

'Precisely,' Sir Alexander sighed, then continued quickly, 'Of course you'll be considered. And Sard. And I suppose each Director will have his own little pet. Oh, the in-fighting will be the epitome of the degradation of man.'

It was at this profundity that the taxi stopped outside the Club Fanfini, now closed and looking rather shabby.

'There's my car,' Clarron announced with a great sense of relief, even joy.

But when the taxi carefully drew alongside his face showed only disgust. Three accidents had befallen his pride and the Company's status: one, somebody had vomited all over his near side fender. Two, someone else, or perhaps the same person, had vomited down the off side of his bonnet. Three, yet another person, or the previous two, or perhaps all three together, had vomited over the entire surface of his windscreen.

'I think I'm going to gawk,' announced Sir Alexander Saunders.

'For Christ's sake Alex!' exclaimed Clarron. 'Have you ever seen anything like that in your entire life?'

'No, and I don't wish to again. For one thing, that car is not going to be driven to the office in its present state. What an image-maker for a giant Corporation in the hygiene game!'

*

As the taxi sped on toward the office skyscraper near the

Thames, Saunders grew morose and sullen. 'Ominous, Jules,' he muttered. 'The day has started most ominously. Two hangovers, two cars and a sideboard of china – all in very grievous condition.'

'Well, we can clear up one of those for a start,' Clarron said with a painful attempt at cheerfulness, trying to bolster the sagging morale of the mighty Saunders. 'I'll send one of the office boys out to clean the car up, then bring it round to the office.'

'Not sound, old boy,' Saunders mumbled. 'Office boys are the very root of slander, rumour and gossip. We'll have to send somebody with his head screwed on. Somebody sound, resourceful, discreet.'

'Not me,' Clarron confessed. 'I'd be puking as fast as I wiped it up.'

'I can understand that all right. But who can we send?' Saunders mused. 'Someone we can really rely upon. Someone . . . ah, I have it – Sard. I don't suppose Reg will like the mopping up a bit too much. But he's the very man for the job. Dependable chap, old Reg.'

*

The taxi dropped them at the skyscraper and both men wearily made their way to their respective offices. Clarron's secretary, well trained in the ways of executive initiative, was already replying to his correspondence. Meanwhile, in the ante-room to the Managing Director's office, Saunders found his secretary typing madly. As he entered she stopped and spoke briskly:

'Three internal memos for you this morning, Sir. And a report from our Midland headquarters. They're on your desk.'

'Thank you,' Saunders replied and marched to the door of his office. But his secretary stood up and spoke to him in rather a high voice:

'Sorry, Sir. I have some bad news for you.'

'Bad news?' asked Saunders and peered at her from under deeply hooded eyes.

'Yes, Sir. I'm afraid you won't have the morning free.'

'Really?' replied Saunders, and he observed that his secretary looked awfully like some WRAF officer about to tell him that the Dambuster mission had failed.

'Yes, Sir,' she continued. 'Mr Gold has been on. Three of his ultra-violet purifying machines have broken down. 'He'll be here in twenty minutes. To see you.'

'Oh no. No, no, no. Absolutely not! Hell! No! God! What? Twenty minutes, you say? Christ. Get Sard. Tell him to go to the Club Fanfini. No. Look up the street, only mention the street. Company car there to be cleaned and returned to the pool. This is to be done discreetly. Di-screet-ly. Get Clarron. I want him in my office immediately.'

With this the Managing Director crashed into his private office, slammed the door behind him and staggered, arms outstretched, to the cocktail cabinet on the far side of the room He was gulping a large vodka when Clarron entered.

'Trouble, sir?'

'Trouble! Jules, all hell is breaking loose. Pour yourself a drink – we must straighten ourselves out. Fast. The walls are crumbling, Jules. The centre cannot hold and mere anarchy is about to be loosed upon the world. Goldilocks is on his way here. Three purifying machines – at £20,000 each – they're on the blink.'

'And Goldfinger's on the dry?'

'Precisely.'

Now Saunders did something which was recognisable instantly to Clarron – or, for that matter, is equally familiar to anyone who has ever rushed the morning drink. His lips puckered. His nostrils dilated. Sweat burst across his brow. Staring straight ahead at some non-existent object he slowly lowered his glass to the table. Julius had already opened the door to the private bathroom adjoining the office and stood to one side as Sir Alexander Saunders rushed in. 'Aaar, aaar,' the great man shouted down the lavatory bowl. 'Ahooh! Aaar, aaaaaaaaaaaa*guglegoosh!*'

After a few moments silence, followed by the flushing of the lavatory and the running of cold water, Saunders reappeared mopping his face with a large white towel. 'Damn,' he growled.

'All that good work gone to waste.' But Clarron had already poured him a new drink.

'Excellent fellow. Must treat this one with respect. Now then,' and Sir Alexander attempted some recovery, 'what in the name of hell are we going to do about this bitchy, disgustingly sober Gold?'

'Suggestion,' Clarron offered. 'You've been called to Home Office for urgent consultation.'

'Not sound,' opined Saunders. 'If Gold doesn't see me, whatever the reason, he'll assume I'm on the thrash. And you know what these buggers are like when they go off the booze. And Gold, being one of the heaviest drinkers I've ever met has, in sobriety, turned into the most aggressively puritanical bastard imaginable. God,' Saunders went on, 'I can remember the days when he used to get so plastered that he actually begged me, in all seriousness, to produce a machine for purifying his own blood stream.'

Neither man came up with any brilliant stroke for dealing with the dreaded Gold and it was decided that Sir Alex would have to take the inevitable caning. However, it was further decided that Clarron was to cancel all engagements for the day and to stand by, in a sort of ad lib role, in case some idea should come to Saunders during the gruelling hours ahead.

*

When Mr Gold did arrive he did not wait to be announced. Instead he marched straight into the Managing Director's office, threw his large black hat on to an empty chair, and proceeded to tear off his astrakhan coat.

'Ah Leo,' announced Saunders heartily, for a further six Vodkas had returned him to something approaching his normal state of health. 'How very pleasant to see you. Do sit down and explain this appalling news my secretary mentioned to me.'

'Alex,' stated Gold with uncontrolled viciousness, throwing his coat on to another empty chair, 'I've known you a long time now. Good friends. O.K. We do good business togther.'

Thus started what was to prove to be one of the most harrowing, painful, nerve-racking and totally destructive hours in the long and illustrious career of one of Britain's captains of industry. Gold whispered about implied agreements, he shouted about contractual clauses, he screamed about loss of profits and foamed on endlessly about bad faith, inefficiency and downright dishonesty. Saunders threw in a few 'ifs' and 'buts' but nothing, it seemed, could stop the flow of ungrammatical Central European invective which Gold sprayed into the face of the man, who, Gold now seemed to be implying, had allowed alcohol to come between the interest of his own Company and that of its largest client. With diabolical logic and damning statistics pouring into his ears Saunders was not able to point out that everything had been all right when Gold was drinking and that it was therefore the *lack* of alcohol which had led to the breakdown in their relationship.

However, the ordeal was temporarily relieved by a buzz on Saunders' intercom. Summoning up the last vestiges of authority he answered it peremptorily.

'Yes. What is it?'

'I'm sorry to disturb you, Sir Alexander,' came the nervous voice of his secretary. 'It's urgent. Could you come into my office?'

With a profound sense of relief Saunders replied, not too strongly:

'I *am* with Mr Gold, you know.'

'I realise, Sir. This is urgent.'

With a stoical frown Saunders excused himself and marched into his secretary's office.

'Oh you darling,' he sighed once he had closed the door. 'What timing,' and he mopped his brow with a pristine handkerchief. 'Just a couple of minutes respite and I might be able to deal with this ogre.'

'I'm sorry, Sir,' his secretary said hesitatingly. 'There is an emergency.'

'Emergency?' Saunders queried, fear once again returning to his blinking eyes.

'Yes, Sir,' she began. 'The basement is flooding.'

'Don't be so damned silly!'

Saunders thought very hard for a long moment and then asked:

'Well, can't the maintenance men deal with it?'

'They refuse,' came the ominous answer.

'Refuse?' blurted Saunders.

'Yes Sir,' she explained. 'Apparently the main sewers have backed up.' Saunders was sinking into a chair, his head in his hands, as she continued. 'Vouchers department is already flooded. Current invoice department is flooding at the moment. All the other offices have had to be evacuated.'

'And Golddigger on the premises,' he moaned. 'Too much. This is simply too much for one mere human to stand.' Saunders seemed to weave slightly in his chair, then asked to be put through to Mr Clarron.

'J . . . J . . . Jules,' he stuttered into the phone. 'Get down to my secretary's office immediately. And Jules, bring something to drink.'

'No Vodka up here. Have to be gin.'

'Good God, man. I don't care if it's liquid fuel for bloody rockets – I need a drink!'

It seemed an eternity, an eternity during which Saunders imagined the smell of sewage to be permeating throughout the building and nauseating Mr Gold, before Clarron arrived – complete with bottle.

When they had each taken a heavy draught from the bottle, watched by an expressionless secretary, Saunders explained the situation and asked Clarron for his advice.

'The obvious, I suppose. Send for the plumbers.'

'Not sound,' commented Saunders irritably. 'Just imagine Goldfinch in there witnessing a lot of plumbers, not to say the fire brigade itself, pumping a battleshipfull of sewage bilge out of our front door. No,' Saunders announced, 'two things must be done immediately. Gold must be removed. And someone must fight the disaster – the maintenance men won't go near it.' After another swig from the bottle Saunders added: 'And I just don't see how *I* could get Gold-dust out. He's tearing my ears off. Now pour a stiff one into yourself, Jules, and perhaps one of us will come up with something.'

Julius had finished his second mouthful when he put forward his suggestions – solutions which now, in the whole of his health, seemed so obvious and yet, at the same time, not entirely lacking in gifted inspiration, in tact, force, subtlety.

'One – your secretary tells Gold your mother has just had a heart attack and you're so upsct you've rushed off to the hospital. Two – she tells him I'll be down in a minute to act on your behalf. Three – I immediately whisk Goldburger off to lunch.'

'Good,' Saunders nodded. 'Very good. *But what about my new liquid fertilizer unit spreading all over my lower ground floor?*'

'Well,' said Clarron thoughtfully and conspiringly. 'As Managing Director you're bound to feel that your place is on the bridge of this listing ship, not in the torn bowels.'

'Too true, my good man. Too bloody true. But who will we get? Someone who can really take charge, stop confusion, get things done. Someone of proven ability in this kind of situation, someone who . . .' Saunders paused, the solution registering visibly on his brows. 'Ah, Sard. The very man,' and he turned to his secretary. 'Sard back yet?'

'Yes, Sir, he brought the car back about an hour ago.'

'Splendid,' boomed Saunders, and what with the drink and Clarron's suggestion, he was indeed returning to his former self. 'Get Sard down there.' he ordered his secretary. 'He's to handle the situation on his own – no brigade, no fuss. Then tell Merrygold about my aged mother. Then you, Jules, take over. Personally, I'm disappearing.'

*

The next four hours went exactly as planned. Julius Clarron and Mr Gold had lunch at an exorbitantly expensive Italian restaurant in Knightsbridge. Julius was as helpful as possible, bearing in mind that he was not fully conversant with Mr Gold's account – but that was not to say that he wouldn't take full responsibility for anything said during their talk and for any executive action following from it. At the same time he quite understood how upset Mr Gold was by what appeared to be slackness on the part of the Company, but what might turn out to be nothing more than lack of good liaison, for which some lower minions in either Company might be held responsible; but the main point was that the units themselves were sound and the service was of a standard to be expected from a top professional organisation. In any case, perhaps Mr Gold would care for a drink – just to unwind a bit after what must have been an exhausting morning. No, Mr Gold wasn't drinking these days. Clarron pointed out that he wasn't suggesting drinking as such, simply a therapeutic imbibition to relieve nervous tensions before they sat down to what promised to be an excellent meal. On second thoughts Mr Gold could see no harm in just one whisky to get the old digestive juices going. In returning the round Mr Gold said he felt completely relaxed in the company of Mr Clarron and perhaps they should have a large one to cement their most sympathetic relationship. When they had finished this, Clarron announced that he refused to go back on to small ones as this seemed a retrograde step. When Mr Gold's round came up again he fell in with the spirit of the whole thing and boldly ordered triples. Clarron followed suit and informed the head-waiter that they were not yet ready to eat but to hold the table. Then Mr Gold wagered Clarron five pounds that, he, Clarron, was unable to drink three triples in one minute. Clarron made damned sure he lost by about four seconds and so was in a position to ask for a chance to get his money back. Would Mr Gold drink three triples in one minute? Gold lost by fifteen seconds but thought the whole game to be damned good bloody fun, O.K.

*

Meanwhile, Sir Alexander Saunders was at the bar of his club, chatting aimiably to a Parliamentary Under-Secretary and consuming large numbers of a particularly vicious cocktail known as 'Death in the Afternoon'. They decided to lunch together, and with their melon they ordered a bottle of rather dry Hayder Riesling '63. This they found a bit sharp but with a feminine personality all its own. With the smoked salmon they tried a bottle of Laferte Chablis '61. This was sterner stuff altogether and they consumed it with gusto. When it came to their Veal Cordon Bleu they broke the rules audaciously and went for a Chateauneuf du Pape '59. This proved to be such an unexpected success that they ordered a second bottle. By now feeling rather mellow and somewhat bold they demanded from the wine waiter that their strawberries and cream be accompanied by nothing less than a bottle of Baron Phillipe de Rothschild Agnew Blanc 1917. And when they discovered, over the stilton, that their port was Cockburn '50 they insisted that a bottle of this be produced immediately. Of course the waiter knew how Sir Alexander liked to finish his meal, and duly produced coffee well laced with French peasant brandy.

*

Meanwhile, back at the office, Reg Sard was doing some really splendid work. With a truly magnificent sense of Company loyalty he had jumped straight into the three feet of water covering the basement. (Water? Let us describe it a little more accurately as a fluid containing semi-solid substances.) With heroic might and the use of several filing cabinets plus the contents thereof, he had stemmed the all but annihilating torrent. Thus, as Saunders returned to his office for a short nap before the four o'clock Board Meeting, and as Mr Gold, tagliatelle on lapel and his arm around Clarron's shoulder, was explaining that his own Company was full of dumb clucks who probably didn't know how to use the new machines properly, the industrious Mr Sard, looking like a cross between Charlie Chaplin and a pot-holer who had just made a ghastly mistake, could be seen moving stealthily, sloppy bucket in hand, toward the Corporation manhole in the Company's parking lot.

*

The Board Meeting proved to be a surprisingly simple and successful affair. From beginning to end it was dominated by a robust and forceful Saunders – a man who, now in the whole of his health and exercising that aggressive authority which only alcohol plus a well-developed Asmolian Syndrome can produce, was not to be crossed. The transcript of this meeting makes most interesting reading and I give it to you now verbatim.

MANAGING DIRECTOR: Well, gentlemen, we all know why we're here. Now in the normal course of events we would no doubt have a lengthy discussion on the matter, followed by the proposing of several candidates to the Board, followed by a vote – and no doubt, I fear, many votes. Now you all know how I hate using bulldozing techniques at our meetings. It is my well-known policy to encourage open and confidential discussion and to stand by any majority vote. However, today's decision is a rather unique one, and the circumstances surrounding it are *quite* unique. For this reason I intend to make a strong proposal immediately. When I've explained my reasons for this proposal I have not the slightest doubt that you will agree whole-heartedly with me, thus simplifying and shortening this meeting considerably.

Let me start by saying that this has been a particularly trying day, not only for myself, but for the firm as a whole. My entire day, which was pretty heavily booked anyway, was thrown completely out of joint by our biggest client and my personal account – Mr Gold. The Gold account, at the best of times, is involved and complex. Under normal conditions Leo himself is not too bad. But for some reason best known to himself – Gold went on the dry.

DIRECTOR: I'd heard that.

DIRECTOR: Yes, so had I. In fact I saw him at a cocktail party last week. The blighter was drinking Coca-Cola. Looked a real twit, I can tell you.

MANAGING DIRECTOR: Well I'm very glad to announce from information just received on the telephone, that that sorry state of affairs is over. Gold is at this moment totally canned at some Dago hash-house in Knightsbridge.

DIRECTOR: Oh, well done, Sir!

DIRECTOR: Yes, indeed. Congratulations.

MANAGING DIRECTOR: As a matter of fact the congratulations must go to someone else. The point is that Gold arrived at my office this morning, unannounced, and viciously sober. He attacked me, the firm, my integrity and our efficiency. It was a sickening sight. However, during his ravings I had an intuitive feeling that he'd behave a lot better if he was dealing with one of our senior execs. instead of with me personally. So I pulled in Clarron and let the two of them get on with it. Well, Clarron's just been on the phone to me. In what I can only describe as executive brilliance, he has pulled a three point stroke which has Gold eating out of our hands. One: he's got him off the wagon and back to the world of civilised human and business relationships. Two: there is to be an officer appointed – at their expense, mind you – to liaise between our two companies. Three: our books relating to the Gold account are to be open for inspection by Gold himself, thus allaying any fears he may have about exorbitant profit.

DIRECTOR: Excuse me, Sir, but surely it *is* exorbitant. If I remember correctly the net profit on the Gold account covers the overheads of our entire organisation.

MANAGING DIRECTOR: No fear there. I'm going to propose that Clarron takes over the account, and by the time Clarron is through with the books they'll be cooked to the point of combustion. And having Jules handle the account will leave me more time to handle the ever increasing complexities of laying down general policy. Naturally, of course, whoever handles the Gold account must be on the Board and it follows that Jules must be appointed immediately.

DIRECTOR: And what about Reg Sard, Sir? He's one of our best men.

MANAGING DIRECTOR: He is indeed. One of our very best. Which brings me to even more tribulations of the day. Some hooligan befouled one of our cars during the night and Reg dealt with the embarrassing situation admirably. Also the sewers packed up today.

DIRECTOR: Good Lord! I didn't know anything about this.

MANAGING DIRECTOR: And I trust no one ever will. We'd be the laughing stock of the country. However, I think that between us Reg and I have the situation well under control. There'll be no need to call in outside help. Once again Reg has proved himself to be the kind of man one can turn to in any emergency. Which brings me to this point: I feel it's time Reg was given more responsibility. I am definitely of the opinion that in Sard we have the classic position of 'the right man in the right place'. So let's leave him there. At the same time, Clarron cannot possibly be expected to handle the Gold account along with his present accounts – to say nothing of his extre responsibilities as a Director. So the obvious solution is to hand over Clarron's existing accounts to Sard.

DIRECTOR: Brilliant!

DIRECTOR: And so simple.

DIRECTOR: Trust you to cut the Gordian knot, Sir.

DIRECTOR: Hear, hear.

MANAGING DIRECTOR: Well then, gentlemen, let's vote. Jules Clarron to take over the Gold account and be appointed as of now to the Board: Reg Sard to stay where he is and take over all Clarron's existing accounts.

COMPANY SECRETARY: By a show of hands this motion is carried unanimously.

MANAGING DIRECTOR: Excellent. Now then, let's adjourn to my private office and have a drink to this. We can also phone Jules and Gold and give them the good news.

And so the gaggle of Directors followed Sir Alexander to his office where copious libations were imbibed. It was while they were waiting for the call to Clarron that Sir Alexander put in casually:

'I'll have a word with Reg tomorrow and explain things to him. I dare say he's pretty busy at the moment. Actually, now that we're in private I don't mind saying, just among ourselves, mind you, that excellent and extremely sound fellow that Sard may be there's something about him, somethng I can't put my finger on, which makes me feel he's not really Director material.'

'I'm glad you yourself mentioned that, Sir,' said one of the Directors as he polished off his second drink. 'I've often had the same feeling. We're lucky to have him, of course. But there's something negative about Reg. He's not really very outgoing, if you know what I mean.'

'I do indeed,' replied Saunders.

'Actually, Sir,' said another Director, 'I think you put your finger on it when you said that he's the right man in the right spot so let's leave him there.'

The telephone rang. Saunders answered it and boomed down the line.

'Congratulations, Jules! You're now a Director. Yes, unanimous vote, old boy. And what's more, Jules, you can tell Goldplate there that you'll be handling his account from now on – *exclusively*. And you can tell him we heartily endorse the suggestions you've made. What? Pretty boiled, is he? Excellent. Keep up the good work. Tell you what, Jules, why don't we all have a little celebration – you, Gold, the whole lot of us? What's that? Oh, splendid idea! Yes, indeed! I'll leave it to you then. Book the whole gang of us in at the Club Fanfini.'

*

Well, that, more or less, is the end of the story. Far be it from me to draw any obvious conclusions. Perhaps it would be better to sum up the day's events, take stock of the situation as we leave it, and hazard a guess at what the future holds.

> Throughout the day Sir Alexander Saunders did little but drink his loaf off. True, he did have an unpleasant hour or so with Gold, but this was more than compensated for by unloading the account in the afternoon.
>
> Julius Clarron, likewise, did nothing but loop himself utterly. Added to this he was appointed to the Board and was unburdened of all his accounts and given the biggest in the Company.
>
> Reginald Sard, for his part, spent the day scrubbing

puke off cars and mucking around in sewage. For his efforts he has been repaid with the added burden of the Clarron accounts, plus an assured future of utter mediocrity.

As we leave the story Sard, covered from head to toe in defecatory matter, has reduced the flood level to a three inch layer of sludge, with which he is filling his 1,223rd bucket: at the same time, atop a table in Club Fanfini, Jules Clarron is demonstrating the more violent aspects of the Inca war dance, ably abetted by his enthusiastic partner, Mr Leopold Gold.

The future seems pretty obvious.

Sir Alexander Saunders will become Chairman – a position in which he will do no work whatsoever and in which he will entertain those politicians and those clients whose company he finds affable. Reginald Sard, being a sound man who is in the right position will remain in that position, collecting ever more accounts as they are dropped by the rising luminaries, until the day he collects his gold watch, which will no doubt be given to him by the then Managing Director, that man of vision and enterprise, the symbol of all that is best in British industry and power – the illustrious Sir Julius Clarron.

*

ADDENDUM

From article in *This Week* magazine, dated November 5, 1970.

HELPING TO DRY OUT

One of the most enlightened approaches by industry towards the problem of the alcoholic employee is that which was adopted in 1965 by the Bethlehem Steel Corporation, the huge American consortium of companies.

Bethlehem, realising that the typical alcoholic is talented and intelligent and that an attempt to salvage him, both on economic and humanitarian grounds, seemed much better than firing him, launched a corporation-wide alcoholic programme built on rehabilitation to counter the problems created by alcoholic employees. Each employee with a drinking problem was urged to seek help through the plan.

The programme has worked so well that last week Bethlehem took the somewhat unusual step of advertising its success in the leading American magazines. They claimed proudly that 60% of those who enrolled for 'drying out' had made 'dramatic progress.'

The corporation claims that there's 'a better than even chance' that the problem drinker can be saved from his affliction.

'We hope,' announced Bethlehem, 'that we are seeing the dawn of a day when every business and every citizen views the alcoholic for what he is: sick, but not sickening.'

So maybe all big American businesses aren't so heartless after all. Either that or the alcoholic elements on the payroll must really be the people with the ability.

Probably the latter.

*

No comment, except perhaps to the Bethlehem Steel Corporation of America that, though their findings are correct, their decisions are directly opposed to Asmolian principles and further, if they continue to dry out their executives, they would be well advised to start selling their own stock.

Early Days at the Institute

Ladies and Gentlemen: In my talk to you today I would like to tell you something about our early days at the Institute. And I suppose the first point to discuss is the inception of the Institute itself. No doubt many of you have been reading the garbled and grossly exaggerated reports in the press concerning the Estate of the late Mr Ezekeal Linkfelder and how, it is alleged, that I, under false pretences, swindled the Trustees of that Estate into handing over a vast sum of money. It has also been said that the Institute is a hotbed of alcoholism and sexual excess. It is further alleged that the Institute is a dipso factory turning out about a hundred confirmed drunkards a year. Now these are highly emotional phrases and almost entirely meaningless. I think a dispassionate examination of the facts would be a far better way of clarifying the position between the Trustees and myself . . . or should I say the erstwhile Trustees and myself.

*

It was a gloriously hot August day in 1969, one of those days when all the pretty girls in the world seem to be strolling through Kensington Gardens, a day when London's wealth seems to express man's noblest and simplest ambitions, a day when the pubs are a haven of quiet refreshment and God is securely ensconced in His heaven. As was my regular practice in those days, I was quietly perusing the official lists of registered charities. For years I had dreamed of having my own research institute and of carrying out what I felt to be the most significant achievement of which I was capable – namely, a completely fresh start to the study of alcohol. It was on this auspicious day that I discovered the Trust fund set up by Mr Ezekeal Linkafelder. And I knew immediately that the marriage between my unique ambition and the unique Will of Mr Linkafelder would prove fruitful in the extreme.

Thus it was, having put my ideas to paper and having clarified my intentions in every detail that I approached the Trustees – a two man firm of Solicitors in the City – with my proposition.

Mr Ezekeal Linkafelder (who stipulated that under all conditions and for all time he was to remain anonymous) was an extremely wealthy industrialist and influential adviser to the Government. It appears that he blew the greater part of his lolly while drinking himself to death, his final demise being under the most compromising circumstances in the bridal suite of a major West End hotel. Although he had at his command the services of a whole bevy of Solicitors, Counsel and legal advisers, he had chosen to draw up his last Will and Testament himself. This was to prove unfortunate for his Trustees; for wise man though he was, he was no great shakes at legal terminology.

He was also unfortunate in his choice of Trustees. Eschewing all his colleagues and advisers, he chose two elderly Solicitors who had been at school with him – and he chose them for the simple reason (Oh! the folly of it) that he had never known them to take a drink in their lives. The misguided thinking behind this decision becomes apparent when one looks at the terms of the Will. All his worldly goods and chattels, his Holdings and investments were to be realised and formed into a Trust Fund. This Fund was to be invested in blue-chip equities to be chosen by his Trustees (the only proviso being that not a penny should be invested in any distillery or brewery shares or the shares of Companies engaged in the distribution or sale of liquor). The income from the Trust was to go to his wife during her lifetime, after which the entire Capital Account was to be given over to research into the effects of alcohol on the human system.

Well, the wife passed on a few minutes after being informed of the circumstances under which old Zeke had popped it, and for five years the Trustees had been unable to find any person or organisation to which they could give the money, bearing in mind the *exclusive* nature of the work to which it was to be put. Thus when I approached them, late in 1969, with my unique suggestion for an Institute which was to start again at the very beginning of research into alcohol and its relation to human behaviour, they knew that at last they had found their man.

The formalities were extremely simple and straight-forward. The Trustees, hounded by distant relatives in Australia and plagued almost out of practice by every Institution, University and crank in the country, were only too pleased to settle the matter as quickly as possible. A document was drawn up which made me sole Trustee and gave me complete discretion as to how the money was to be spent, provided it was used within the framework of the original Will. This document has vindicated me in every court of law into which the rubbery old gentlemen have since dragged me – accusing me of using the money to ends diametrically opposed to the wishes of the late Mr Linkafelder. However, as the courts have pointed out, the Trustees are not justified in assuming that Mr Linkafelder would or would not approve of how his money is being spent; and secondly, I can hardly be held personally responsible for the revolutionary discoveries which are the direct result of using Mr Linkafelder's money as he instructed it to be spent. So much for the turbulent Trustees.

So it was that I woke up one morning in February 1970 with a sizeable amount of money at my disposal – the nice round sum of four hundred and thirty three thousand, six hundred and fifty two pounds, fourteen shillings and seven pence, minus Stamp Duty.

*

The premises of the Institute stand in their own grounds of three acres in a London suburb. The original building was erected at the end of Queen Victoria's reign and was at that time meant as a Home for stray animals in need of shelter and sustenance. It is a vast L-shaped single-storey horror which was later used to facilitate mental patients in transit to more secure quarters. During the last decade several attempts have been made to convert it into a light engineering works, but planning permission had always been refused because there is no road to the grounds, merely a winding and tortuous path.

On taking up residence, I immediately initiated a programme of expansion and internal reconstruction. Central heating was installed and my own quarters were decorated and furnished. The section previously used for the housing of stray animals was extended and various cubicles were built for the purpose of experimentation. The section which at one time held captive the misfits of society was also extended and converted into living quarters for staff and patients. Within a remarkably short period all was finished – including the outside building now known as Ward D. Alone, but full of enthusiasm, I conducted my first great experiment.

Jasper and Henry had been with me for a long time. As cats go they are really very ordinary. Jasper is a rather large black beast with quite a temper and very strong ideas about what is best for him and what is not. Henry, a smaller grey cat, is really rather affectionate with humans but tends to stay out of Jasper's way whenever possible. It is not that they actively dislike each other, it is more a question of differing personality types. Jasper gets what he wants by use of tooth and claw; Henry does not often get what he wants but manages to lead a peaceful life.

The fundamental questions that were bothering me at this time were along the following lines:

Why does one person turn to drink and not another?

Under what circumstances does a person *prone* to drink actually *take* to drinking?

And what are the effects of alcohol, over a sustained period, on a person prone to its consumption?

As a start to finding some of the answers to these questions I removed Jasper and Henry from my quarters and installed them together in Cubicle One of the experimental section.

Cubicle One is a bare room with one naked light bulb hanging from the ceiling. In one corner there is a dirt-box. In another, a door. In the third is a small floor level hatch through which food is introduced and empty saucers removed. In the fourth corner is a peep-hole and a wide angle lens for closed-circuit television.

Jasper and Henry were reduced to one communal saucer of milk per day. For the first week this worked out reasonably well. Once the saucer of milk had been pushed through the hatch, Jasper would trot up and have his fill. When he had consumed ample sufficiency he would stretch, yawn and move off slowly. Now Henry, seeing that Jasper had no further interest in the milk, would move forward tentatively to the saucer, occasionally casting a reassuring glance behind, and greedily finish off whatever may have been left. When the saucer was empty he would slink away to that part of the room which was at the time farthest removed from Jasper.

At the beginning of the second week I introduced a saucer containing two-parts milk, one-part gin. Jasper as usual trotted immediately to his accustomed nosh-up. This time, however, he did not dive straight in. He sniffed the milk, obviously did not care for it and moved around to the other side of the saucer. Another experimental sniff and a tentative lick confirmed that this was not proper fare. After a few moments he returned to his corner, his tail twitching. Henry, assuming that Jasper had finished, slunk up to the saucer. His reactions were much the same as those of Jasper, and soon he too had returned to his corner, where he just sat.

It was a full hour later that little Henry, keeping a steady eye on the recumbent Jasper, again approached the saucer. This time he tried a few licks and sneezed. A second attempt seemed more successful, though he had to keep his eyes closed. After several more attempts he seemed quite reconciled to his new drink, though he often had to stop for long pauses, during which he breathed very heavily. After about twenty minutes or so he stopped drinking altogether and just stood there – simply stood looking straight ahead. Then suddenly he careered madly away, running across the room and pouncing on what could only have been an imaginary mouse. The rodent obviously escaped, for little Henry was now running around the room, jumping, pouncing, dancing sideways and occasionally growling. During one headlong flight in pursuit of the wily mouse, he crashed straight into a wall but seemed not to notice. Eventually he came to rest in the centre of the room and again adopted his motionless stance and stared straight ahead. After about half a minute in this position he wheezed heavily and collapsed unconscious to the floor.

Jasper witnessed all this with a frown of deepest suspicion. He relaxed, however, when Henry passed out, and I took this opportunity to slip in a bowl of ordinary milk which Jasper polished off at great speed. He then went over and sniffed at the prostrate Henry, but obviously found the smell of him quite distasteful. He returned to his corner and slept for a few hours.

Ladies and Gentlemen, I don't know how many of you, in your time, have ever seen a badly hungover cat. It is a sight not easily dismissed from one's memory. Henry lay on his side with his lower jaw sagging on the floor. From out of his mouth hung a rather stiff tongue, its colour changed from lively pink to one not dissimilar to old dried blood. His eyes, it is true, were wide open, but they were motionless and bone dry in their sockets. And his first attempts, amid much wheezing, to obtain an upright position, were frankly laughable. And when he did achieve the vertical, he could do nothing but simply stand there. He obviously decided that this was a painful waste of time and he gently, ever so gently, lowered himself to the floor, there to await his final release from this mortal coil.

*

For the next fourteen days Jasper continued to refuse the high octane milk (he soon realised that he would be fed separately later on) and Henry went on his nightly jags. It was during the third week, however, that Henry began to undergo a visible change in behaviour. For one thing, his tendency to sleep nearer and nearer the food hatch eventually resulted in his passing out against the hatch itself. And if he should happen to be in the dirt-box when the spiked milk was introduced, he would hastily leave undone those things which ought to be done and streak bullet-like for the saucer of liquid euphoria. Please remember that during this time Jasper continued to smell the milk each night; and it is because of this habit that, on the twentieth evening, a most interesting and significant phenomenon did occur.

On this occasion I introduced the milk in the ordinary way. Henry had long since given up his role of second fiddle on this matter and both cats approached the saucer at the same time. Henry was there first, and as Jasper arrived, he hunched himself and gave Jasper an unmerciful clout behind the right ear. Jasper was about to retaliate when he found himself being dragged across the room by his left ear. His head was bashed against the wall and he was left in a dazed condition. Henry returned to the joy-juice. No doubt Jasper felt that as he did not want the spiked milk anyway he would leave the matter lie. It was to prove his Munich.

From that moment on, Henry became quite irresponsibly aggressive. If Jasper, quite mystified by this turn of events, attempted to approach the gin he was viciously bitten. Later, when Henry would be well plastered, Jasper would have to suffer totally unprovoked bashings from his snarling room-mate. Over the course of the next few weeks their original relationship was utterly reversed. Jasper, confused by events, tended to stay out of the way of the warring, drunken, feline viking: Henry, when hungover, was completely self-centred and, when cornered, a beast with the most sadistic tendencies.

Of course, looking back now, with hindsight and with the results of thousands of experiments at our disposal, we know that in the case of Jasper and Henry, a naturally inhibited subject, unconsciously suffering from suppressed feelings of unjustified inequality, did, with the means of libido-releasing catalyst alcohol, free himself from his social prison and effect a most fitting revenge on his immediate social circle. This is one of the great joys and universal truths of alcohol – you may not be a Napoleon, but drink enough of his brandy and you soon will be.

*

It was at about this time that Miss Agatha Huntington came to see me. I must explain that for some while I had been running small advertisements in the Statesman and in the Spectator. You know the sort of thing: appealing for intelligent, well-educated people with highly developed social consciences to help, on a voluntary basis, in social work of major significance. Well, Agatha Huntington personified the perfect applicant. She was about forty at the time, bookish, well-dressed, a school teacher who felt that she had more to give than her present job demanded. And *give* she certainly did – but more about that later.

Agatha found the whole idea of the Institute 'tremendously sensible' and agreed to join at once. I have a tape recording of her interview – as I have of all interviews – and I was refreshing my memory the other day when I ran across this little cameo. I had been asking Agatha a few questions about her social life.

PROFESSOR ASMOL: And do you drink, Miss Huntington?

MISS AGATHA HUNTINGTON: Oh yes, When dining out – with friends, you know – I do so enjoy a sherry before the dinner.

PROFESSOR: Sherry. Before some formal dining. Yes, Miss Huntington, but the phrase 'to drink', or 'a drinker', has connotations not strictly limited to the odd sherry before dinner. In any case – dry or sweet?

MISS HUNTINGTON: Dry or sweet what?

PROFESSOR: Sherry, Miss Huntington. I'm trying to ascertain whether your preference is for dry or sweet sherry.

MISS HUNTINGTON: Well, you know, Professor Asmol, I'm not too good at ordering. The barmen do seem to be so frightfully busy, don't they? I usually leave such matters –dry or sweet, did you ask? – I like to leave such matters to one of the gentlemen. If you must write something down on that form, I suppose medium would be the best answer.

PROFESSOR: Thank you, Miss Huntington. Most helpful of you. There is another question I'd like to ask you. No need for involved detail or anything like that. Tell me – do you know the hours during which the public houses are open in London?

MISS HUNTINGTON: Well, now, Professor. They're open during the day, aren't they. Then at night they close sometime around ten or eleven. And during the day-time, too, they close for lunch. No, not at lunchtime, of course. So many people go to the pub for lunch, don't they? But sometime in the afternoon – yes, they definitely close then.

From this it will be seen that Agatha did not come to the Institute a craven boozer. But it is the question of pub hours that was to prove so significant and I will be dealing with these when I come to the question of 'Hooking In', or 'Early Signs of Hope'.

During the few days which it took Agatha to move in, the bar at the Institute was completed. It is a form of Cocktail Bar – subdued lighting, background music, snug little fire and expensive carpeting. It differs from other Cocktail Bars only insomuch as there is no charge for the vast supplies of varied alcohol and there are no opening or closing hours. In due course it was to become the most swinging bar in Western Europe.

It was in this bar, some ten days later, that Agatha and I were discussing the complex nature of our work. I had by this time acquired quite a number of cats and was itching (I wouldn't go so far as to say literally) to experiment. As I explained to Agatha:

'What concerns me at the moment, Agatha, is the *type* of person who takes to drink – and in particular the *state* of that person when he actually takes a drink. I mean, how often has one heard people say – "God, I need a drink"? Or – "What I need now is a stiff drink"? It's very much like people who have never smoked asking for a cigarette after a car accident. They're in some sort of state which demands some sort of drug – and some people are more given to this state than others. It's only one facet of drinking, I know. But I can't help feeling it's an important one.'

'Actually,' Agatha told me,' my grandfather couldn't sleep unless he had drunk a bottle of port.' And she added, rather significantly I thought: 'He died in his sleep.'

'Yes, insomnia's a problem we'll have to look into. But it's *types* and *conditions* that interest me at the moment. You take that new cat Harold. Perfectly contented little fellow, well adjusted to his surroundings and seems to be neither disturbed nor upset by anything. He knows what Gin is and what its effects are. Occasionally he tries some. But very, very seldom – and then only in small doses. Whenever he has the choice he prefers straight milk. Now what I want to do is to change that cat! I want somehow to alter his placid make-up. Turn him into a different kind of cat – say a nervous, furtive, apprehensive cat – and see if his attitude to alcohol changes.'

*

It was Agatha who procured the chicken. Just what story she gave the local butcher I do not know. But sure enough, a week later, a large box arrived at the Institute containing a hideous, stinking, squawking, wildly defecating monster of a chicken. Cubicle Four was prepared immediately.

Cubicle Four was another room with one bare electric light. However, instead of a hatch, this room contained two sets of small swinging doors; one set placed in each of two opposite corners. Behind the 'exit' doors I installed a large turning wheel with a crank-handle attached. This gave me a gear ratio of about ten to one. I was thus able to wind in a piece of string at something over fifty-five miles per hour. When Harold was moved into Cubicle Four this piece of string stretched from my wheel, through the 'exit' doors, across the floor and out under the 'entrance' doors on the other side of the room. Harold accepted the piece of string as part of the furniture and never really noticed it. Little did the poor mite realise that this innocent piece of string was to turn his serene world into one of twitching horror.

For three days Harold was given two bowls of milk at each meal. One bowl was strongly spiked with gin. This Harold, as usual, refused. On the fourth day his world changed.

He was sitting peacefully, licking his left paw, when Agatha and I took up our positions. I was at the giant wheel, ready to give it a mighty spin. Agatha, stroking the chicken to keep the miserable thing quiet, was at the back of the 'entrance' doors, attaching the other end of the string to the bird's neck. When all was ready she gave a gentle tug on the string and with total acceleration I turned loose my engine of propulsion.

The results were quite extraordinary. With an horrendous crash a squawking, choking, flapping, half-throttled chicken spun into the room and raced across the floor at terrific speed. It had reached the half-way mark on its gaggling journey when Harold reacted with the most electric intensity – the cat, overwhelmed with terror, jumped an incredible two and a half feet straight into the air. By the time he landed, the chicken had smashed through the 'exit' doors.

Now I know we have all heard expressions about hair standing on end and about being driven up the wall. But both these phenomena now occurred: Harold stood on the floor looking as if he had been plugged into the electricity main socket, his hair stiff and bristling – then he dashed across the room and made heroic attempts, both futile and painful, to scale the bare shining wall.

Harold did not sleep too well that night, and over the course of the next few weeks, with the insane chicken appearing at odd and disturbing intervals, his sleeping habits, and indeed his behaviour in general, became quite erratic. In the end most of his waking life was spent staring with obvious apprehension at the 'entrance' doors. And even when sleeping his fur would sometimes ruffle in sinister movements. But the most important and satisfying aspect of his behaviour was that, after twenty eight days of assault on his nervous system, he began to drink from both bowls of milk. After a further ten days he gave up the straight milk altogether and settled down to a life of alcoholic stupor and endless hangovers, interspersed with the frantic appearances of a screaming chicken.

The end of this experiment was brought about by the death of the chicken. There is a touch of irony in the incident, insomuch as it was Agatha who needed a drink afterwards. I was at my wheel of iron, ready to spin like mad. Agatha had just tied the string to the chicken's neck. There was a little slack in the string, so Aagtha stepped back. I took this movement to be her usual tug on the string, indicating that the chicken was on the ground. And so I spun the wheel with all the force at my command. This, quite simply, tore the head off the chicken and brought it bumping into the room where it dropped off the string.

Now this was just too much for Harold. In his attempts to flee from the sight of the mutilated head he broke down altogether and threw a fit, frothing in all directions, moaning human cries and viciously chewing one of his back legs.

But Agatha, poor dear, was hardly any better. I found her in the bar trying to force brandy down her throat, while from under her arm the still flapping chicken pumped blood all over herself and much of the wall. And when I remarked how pleasant roast chicken would be for tomorrow's lunch she screamed, trembled and drank. It was a full hour (and three-quarters of a bottle) later that I managed to get her to take a bath. However, she was by this time so sloshed she forgot to run the water and spent the next two hours sleeping naked in a dry bath tub.

*

I would be the last to say that we were in any position to draw conclusions from this experiment. We had achieved something, of course; we had in fact taken a subject utterly indifferent to alcohol, and by inducing a state of anxiety, not to say hysterical anxiety, completely changed the subject's relation to alcohol. But, as I say, we could not fit this phenomena into any general scheme or system. Later, we would learn a great deal more about anxiety, and in particular what is known as Low Frustration Threshold. But at the time we could simply catalogue our experiment and await the day when it could take its place as a significant link in a general theory.

Having mentioned Low Frustration Threshold, I suppose now would be as good a time as any to introduce the case history of Mr Hamilton Hamilton, who was to do such splendid work in this sphere.

Hamilton was twenty-nine when he joined the Institute. Like Agatha, he came in reply to my little advertisement. A tall relaxed man, with incredibly good looks and an extremely friendly manner, he seemed the kind of person who would be moderately successful, without any effort, in whatever political party he found most humorous. He had degrees in languages and history, which were of no immediate interest to him – or of value to us. He also had two million pounds.

'How very interesting, Mr Hamilton,' I remarked during the interview. 'An inheritance, I assume.'

'Yes,' he replied. 'Father was an engineer of some sort. Propulsion seemed to be his field. I think he invented the jet engine or something like that.'

'You're not really sure? I mean to say, you have two million pounds and you simply don't know where it came from?'

'Rather academic point, isn't it?' he replied. 'And of little significance compared to the actual two million levers.'

'Admirable outlook,' I agreed. 'We're very keen on realism here. Half the problem of alcohol is caused by airy-fairy thinking. And I suspect that most of the other half is caused by medical theorists writing when badly hungover.'

I then asked Hamilton what attracted him to apply. Surely, I suggested, a man with his qualifications and stupifying wealth . . .

'Frankly,' he interrupted, 'I'm bored. All my money is in Trust, so I can't do anything useful with it. Having the income, some two or three thousand a week, I don't need to work. And I've yet to find a job that has sufficient intrinsic value to attract even a cretin. I'm not much of a socialite and I can't understand the rules of most gambling games. Women I have and enjoy.'

'And drink?' I pressed with beady eye. 'Do you turn to drink in your boredom?'

'Not during boredom. Otherwise I'd never be sober. But I suffer from what's called cyclical indogenous depression. Then I drink.'

'Cyclical indogenous depression,' I repeated. 'Quite a mouthful. And I see you accept the medical term without question. So will I, provided it does not enter into the realm of alcoholic behaviour. If it does, it must be ruthlessly investigated, analysed, redefined if necessary and thrown out of the window if found wanting. We will stop at nothing . . .'

If I remember correctly I went on at some length. Anyway, I think you have the gist of the interview. I'm glad to say Hamilton did join us. And a very considerable contribution he has made to our work. Not only in the field of research: there have been occasions at the Institute when life has been, in a phrase, hectic. And it was on these occasions, no matter how hysterical their nature, that one could always rely on the urbane sanity of Hamilton Hamilton.

*

Another person to join us at this time was a wiry young man by the name of Eamonn Kelly. Eamonn had not read our advertisement – we had neglected to use such media as 'Weekend', 'Tit-bits', and certain Scandinavian publications of a photographic nature.

Eamonn's family had for generations been intimately involved in the pig breeding industry. His ancestral home was situated on a two acre plot of bog water at Ballybugerifnecs, Co. Kerry. It was here that he, his six brothers and nine sisters, had been reared. He had come to London at a tender age to blow up Knightsbridge Barracks but had been diverted from his task by the far more stimulating attractions of the Soho Cubicles, the Bayswater Warrens and the Holland Park Hideaways. What, then, was he doing applying for a position at the Institute?

'Drink!' he informed me succinctly. 'I'm bloody crazy about it. And there's a rumour around London that there's fair gargle to be had here. I'll be your man in any experiment, or even bloody torture, provided it means scooping.'

His idiom was, for the most part, a language the stranger does not know. But his intentions were admirably clear. Here we had a dedicated boozer of no mean proportions, a man who was prepared to submit himself to anything – and the emphasis he placed on the word 'anything' was quite unmistakeable – for the sake of unlimited alcohol.

Several more questions revealed that Mr Kelly not only knew the pub hours in London, but the hours pertaining to any particular borough in London. He did not know the price of such morning papers as *The Guardian, The Express* or *The Times.* He was, however, able to rattle off the prices of ten different beers, three whiskys (two Irish), gin, rum, vodka, sherries, port, vintage port, four brandies, Madeira, Pernod (both '45' and '90'), Dubonnet, Martini, two Ciders, Benedictine, two Champagnes, Chartreuse, seven wines of various countries – including even a Tonic Wine which he said was called Mel-Burn.

'And tell me, Mr Kelly,' I asked, 'which is your particular favourite?'

'Smoke.'

'Smoke?'

'Yeah,' he told me. 'It's not easy to come by, being illegal, don't you know. But several of the clubs have it. They make it up themselves.'

'Out of what, might I ask?' I queried with growing interest.

'Meths, mostly,' he replied casually. 'Then they distil some branded household products – you know, stuff for cleaning silver, paint removers, shoe polish. That sort of thing.'

'Sounds a most efficient cocktail,' I observed. 'But you do realise, don't you, that you stand a very good chance of blinding yourself?'

'Ah, not at all,' and he dismissed the prospect of a sightless lifetime with a wave of his hand. 'We test it first, don't we?'

'Test it, Mr Kelly? Test it?'

'Sure. You take a teaspoon of the stuff. Then you set fire to it and turn the spoon upside down. If the stuff never reaches the ground, it's too strong. But if it's still burning on the floor – you're on the pig's back.'

'And this is your favourite drink?'

'Well, it is as far as money is concerned. If I was stinking rich I'd drink Irish Malt all the time. With, of course, the odd Cape Kennedy Cracker thrown in as a booster.'

'You must tell me immediately,' I asked with excitement – I may even have been stuttering somewhat – 'just what is a Cape Kennedy Cracker?'

'Ah, this is great stuff altogether,' and Eamonn gestured expansively with his arms. 'And as simple as lighting a fuse. It's just two parts pure surgical spirit, and one part liquid benzedrine.'

Mr Kelly, welcome to the Asmolian Institute.'

*

This then was the beginning of the Asmolian Institute. And these were our first fumbling experiments into the realms of alcohol.

In closing this second lecture, I must pay tribute to our first members: to Henry and Jasper and Harold who gave so much under the noblest of all conditions – total ignorance: to the Unknown Chicken who first lit the everlasting flame of sacrifice: to Hamilton Hamilton who gave his money and peace of mind: to Eamonn Kelly who gave what we might refer to as his mind: and to dear Agatha who gave everything, even in the end the ultimate contribution. When her time comes, Heaven itself will have a servant.

4

This Silly Business of Hangovers

Ladies and Gentlemen: Today I would like to talk to you about our first experiments with a human subject. This was, of course, with Eamonn Kelly, the man to whom I referred in my last lecture. Before one can begin to discuss what happened to Kelly, or what went wrong, one has to envisage the concept of 'alco-lergy'. It was some time after the experiments on Kelly that we discovered and defined alco-lergy; and so it might be a good idea now to define for you exactly what it is and how it differs from any other form of drunkeness or alcoholism.

When God was handing out his gifts to all of us he blessed some with innate talents of a biochemical nature which have been denied to the majority. Examples which come easily to mind are lateral thinking, 20/20 vision and hereditary talents. But the most striking and exemplary cases of this accident of birth are to be found in the fields of musical ability and Asmolianism. I refer to 'Perfect Pitch', and 'Alcolergy'.

In the world of musical talent there are those who, with perfect pitch, can name immediately any note played on a piano. Their talent far exceeds the norm; greater in fact than can be measured by degree. They do not need to learn scales nor chords, nor indeed do they, as far as their minds are concerned, need to learn anything very much. The basis of all music, the fundamentals of musical progression, are with them when they are born: it takes only exposure to music to develop this innate talent.

Likewise with the alcolergic. His metabolic system is

'perfect'. Like the ear of our musical example, his blood accepts a drop of alcohol – his first, or any drop of alcohol – to the manner born. No training, no process of learning, no Asmolian practices, no hooking-in, no build up to addiction, no digestive change-over, no psychic re-training – nothing. All is atuned to the purest of fuel. At birth there is an innate programme, an undeveloped system which needs only to come in contact with the developing agent of alcohol, to progressively lead that person beyond the achievements that you and I might expect of even the most thorough Asmolian practices.

I would like here to draw a parallel to a photograph on which you can see nothing until it is developed. It is the positive to which I refer. Here you have a blank piece of paper which is indistinguishable from another piece of blank paper. Put both these pieces of paper into a solution of photograph developer and one will remain blank while the other will begin to show signs of a design. The longer you leave these papers in the developer the more pronounced becomes the difference. In order to get a design on the ordinary paper, it would be necessary for you to remove it from the developer, dry it and stamp an imprint upon it. Not so the developing positive. This requires no more than contact with the developing chemical, and the longer it is left in the developer the more pronounced becomes the image.

Thus it will be seen that those who are alcolergic need no training, need no assistance, need no help even from Asmolianism. All they do require is contact with alcohol, to which, being allergic, they react rather profoundly. The image is, in fact, in their central nervous system, and it is there by biochemical and hereditary imprint. Here at the Institute we may work for quite a few months on a patient and slowly develop in him the necessary ingredients of addiction, fear, intoxication and constant recourse to the blessed drug. However, in the outside world, the alcolergic requires no training and no teaching; no matter what he does, provided he uses the developing agent of alcohol, he will end up addicted, fearful, and gloriously successful in his drinking. (When I use the words 'fear' and 'fearful', please do not in any way be alarmed; such things are well looked after within the system of Asmolianism.)

You can readily understand then that the alcolergic is, for us, not only a leader but also a visible goal towards which we must all strive. Now, in trying to emulate him we cannot succeeded unless we understand two very important things about him: these are the *progressive* nature of his talent – and his hangovers.

If we bear in mind constantly the photographic paper in the developer, it is not too difficult to grasp the progressive nature of his relationship with alcohol. The nature of his hangover is somewhat more difficult to grasp, and having spent a great deal of time on it, we were compelled to formulate some final definition. For it is a form of mental fear and anguish which is not known to the normal drinker.

We have all seen jokes and cartoons concerning a man at the breakfast table with ice-packs on his head and various other trivia concerning his condition. Not so the alcolergic. The alcolergic suffers no hangovers similar, or in any way connected, to those of the normal man. Our definition was given to us by Bartholomew Kent, an alcolergic who came to stay with us for some time. He was good enough to go out into the outside world and repeatedly precipitate upon himself the alcolergic's hangover and to give us his report. Here are his final words from that report:

> Having drunk myself silly for several weeks, Professor, the hangovers began to build up. As I've said before, there is no pain whatsoever, no real physical discomfort, although there is often a certain amount of shaking. It was while I was attempting to cross Knightsbridge, at some very small hour in the morning, that I realised I was standing there with the definition in my head. Although the road was deserted and there was not the slightest possibility of any traffic coming from anywhere, I was afraid – indeed terrifyingly incapable – of crossing the road. I can only offer you this definition, Professor: 'The terror of crossing a deserted street for fear of being run down by low flying aircraft.'

Now the great joy here for Bartholomew Kent, and all men like him, is that this fear can be overcome immediately by the administration of the precise drug, the lack of which is causing the disturbing symptoms – namely alcohol. We have also discovered, in some cases, that should this not be possible, the use of some other drugs similar to alcohol on the nervous system can also be applied. Needless to say the other drugs are those used by the medical profession, and as such are not comparable to the original drug alcohol. Obviously there is little point, if a system needs alcohol, in giving it anything else; but such are the devious ways of the men of medicine.

It is obviously possible, therefore, for us now to speak of the alcoholic in general terms. It is equally obvious, though, because of the progressive nature of his talents, that we can only refer to alcolergics if we bear in mind, at all times, precisely at what stage they now find themselves.

I hope now you can see how ludicrous it is for the general public to refer to alcoholics at large, when in fact there are two sorts and one of these is naturally progressive. To give you some idea of the confusion in the public's mind regarding the various states of alcoholism and alcolergy, here is a small extract from a conversation in a pub. This particular pub is in the West Riding of Yorkshire. It is a large bar, and in it we find a typical Colonel Blimp, a travelling salesman, and the housewife. It was Bartholomew Kent himself who, while on one of his more fantastic information-gathering trips, procured this archetypal cameo.

BARTHOLOMEW KENT: And as we're on the subject of hay mowing in central Yorkshire, I wonder if any of you could give me the correct definition of alcoholism.

COLONEL BLIMP: Dead easy, old boy. Anyone who gets plastered. That's it.

TRAVELLING SALESMAN: I think, really, it's anyone who allows alcohol to affect their job. A little drinking here and there, all right. But if you can't work with it – then you're in trouble.

HOUSEWIFE: Well, really, its anyone who has to drink in the morning. That's when you know you're an alcoholic.

It will be noticed from these remarks that not only do they all differ – they all exclude the speaker. Colonel Blimp obviously feels that he does not get plastered; the salesman feels that alcohol helps him in his work; the housewife obviously doesn't have a sherry until lunch time. So on top of an ignorant thinking and misinformed public, we have the tragic situation of people trying to define a state from which they themselves wish to remain excluded. This indeed is sad and we know who to blame.

In describing the alcolergic we have left out two virtues which, though not as important, should not be overlooked. These are:

In the first place, due to the fact that he has the imprint already in his system, the alcolergic has a predilection for it to be developed.

Secondly, after the image has been developed to any extent, all further development is at very increasing speeds.

This is quite unlike an ordinary film and here our comparison falls down. The alcolergic obviously wins on three major counts. Because his nervous system carries the message in the first place, he wants it developed. Once it is developed, or even begun, it does not undevelop itself. And in the process of developing, the time needed between one stage and the next shortens. We normal men cannot beat this.

*

Let's take a closer look now at this unique hangover to which Bartholomew Kent referred. At first it seems a state to be avoided. Nobody wants to suffer pain. It might even seem that the development of a robust drinking pattern becomes unattractive. This is certainly not the case. It is the unique quality of these hangovers that showed us the sole cure. If Bartholomew Kent was suffering fear, from no discernible object or force, it follows that one doesn't have to deal with forces or events in order to stop that fear. If, for example, he had suddenly developed a phobia for jet aircraft, it would indeed be difficult to know quite what to do. We cannot cancel all air flights simply for Bartholomew – though, even with normal hangovers, it's not a bad idea. If Bartholomew could tell us of one thing that frightened him we could go out and kill it. However it is not an associated fear in Bartholomew's case; *it is a dissociated fear.* It is what we have come to call 'auto-fear'. It is generated inside the central nervous system of the subject; and not surprisingly it is in that system where we find help. If it is a reduction in the alcohol level, after consuming large amounts of it, which leads to this 'auto-fear', surely it is not beyond the wit of any crass pre-medical student to think of a cure. Of course: man's greatest tranquiliser – a stiff belt at the bottle.

Hamilton Hamilton, however, once suggested that this fear, this 'auto-fear', might in fact be residual terror of severe withdrawal symptoms once experienced by the subject at some time in the past. Apart from the fact that no student of Asmolianism should allow himself to suffer severe withdrawal symptoms, it seems a somewhat ludicrous suggestion. Should anybody be in fear, consciously or unconsciously, of an attack of 'withdrawals' the obvious course of action is to avoid any chance of withdrawing. Once again, by being purely scientific, we find that the simplest and the most difficult of life's problems can be solved simply by trotting down to the nearest local and getting on with it. Yet, for some unknown, but certainly insidious reason, those who are paid by us to discharge the responsibilities of education have tried to confuse this simple truth. They have told our children that this is not the case; they have made snide remarks concerning adults who practise it. They, and the pseudo-medics who supply them with quasi-scientific facts, are the corrupters of our society. Who can now seriously wonder why our contemporary youth is in so much trouble with dangerous drugs.

I will not allow myself nor, through me, the Asmolian

Institute, to be drawn into the present controversy surrounding the use of drugs. For us it never was a controversy; it was a clinical problem. We have solved that problem and it is behind us: however, for those who do not know our resolute views on this matter, here they are:

Soft Drugs. *All tranquilisers and stimulants are acceptable to us provided they are used to tranquilise or stimulate the subject and provided they are used in accordance with his* condition – *not his wishes, which may not necessarily be the same thing. For this he must turn to alcohol.*

Marijuana. *Equally acceptable to us for the same reasons as above. Also acceptable as a social tonic. It must be borne in mind, however, that marijuana is not acceptable as a substitute for drink: it lacks too many of the fundamental Asmolian characteristics.*

Hard Drugs. *This is a joke. Someone, somewhere, is having us all on.*

Now that we have reached the question of hangovers, it is of such importance that we should pause to give it some thought. Usually viewed as a horror and a painful experience which should be avoided, the hangover itself might cause many people some worry before venturing forth on Asmolianism. The hangover has no mystery to it; it is a simple phenomenon, and is simply cured. Perhaps it would be best if we now heard the full report from Bartholomew Kent:

My dear Professor,

Many apologies for not reporting to you sooner, and many apologies for not returning to the Institute at all. This letter, in fact, is being written from what I believe to be The West Dublin Asylum for the Insane. You will remember that you sent me forth, so to speak, to ascertain the nature – not to say unique nature – of a hangover for a person such as myself. I did some splendid work, but as you can imagine from the above address, things went wrong. In fact, I have learned a great deal about how Asmolians should conduct themselves in places such as this and would be glad to pass on this informtaion should you require it.

Just to interrupt here for a moment, I must admit that from time to time some of our researchers did end up in peculiar places. Kent's rules for Asylum behaviour are invaluable and will be referred to later on; but to continue with his letter . . .

I set off from the Asmolian Institute in excellent form. You might remember the send-off party . . . perhaps not. In London it was a joy to be with my friends and to talk to them about your work. All thought it was a very good idea, some were deeply moved and might have arrived with you by now. They seemed to think that the North, and in particular Yorkshire, was where one would contract the worst hangover. I disagreed then and still do. For a real dose of Morning Malaria, London is second only to New York.

I asked these experienced gentlemen to try to put into words just exactly what they felt a hangover was. You were quite correct, Professor; for these people found it extremely difficult, and made it obvious that this area is wide open for research. More than one referred to the impossibility of undoing an omelette – and the frustration of the position should the omelette be your own brains. One young gentleman, a Pakistani if I remember correctly, actually suggested that the fluid inside one's spinal column had somehow become pickled or curried. An older woman put forward an idea which seems so remarkable that it might bear looking into.

She pointed out that if you squeeze a bulge at one end of a sausage-shaped balloon, the bulge simply moves along to the other end. She claims that during the night we suffer stomach cramps (and who is to deny it!). In this case the stomach, like a bulge in a long balloon, is squeezed along the alimentary tract, with the result that we wake up with the stomach in the rectum. This easily explains why the functions of the two orifices concerned seem to be reversed. As one man agreed rather crudely . . .

'You're right, Mum. I always knew I was puking shit, but I never realised why I wanted to stick a devilled egg sandwich up my ass.'

I consulted the Salvation Army on the matter, for surely they have some considerable experience in these matters! They put forward, as irrefutable fact, a theory so fundamental as to destroy forever what little faith remains to us of a benign God. In fact, if they are correct, then those who are fortunate enough to be able to weather a hangover have little to fear from Hell itself, and should be advised to stop at nothing in their hedonistic enjoyment of this present life.

For what it is worth, I also visited a large hospital – a considerable section of which is given over to stamping out Asmolianism by manipulation of the 'patient's' personality. They came out with a lot of mumbo-jumbo concerning toxicity, exposed nerve tissue and inflammation of mucous membrane, plus some nonsense concerning adrenal and vitamin insufficiency. As an example of just how wicked this profession can be: one very young doctor was telling me about the intravenous injection of Parentovite and the administration of Corticotropine when a senior doctor told him to 'shut up'. To realise that they have a cure, but are keeping it from humanity, is to know the full extent of their iniquity! If it is the Salvation Army's God which inflicts such apoplexy upon us, then it is surely the Devil himself who, through his organised agents, withholds the cure.

It then occurred to me that I should consult the man who knows, more than any other, just what constitutes a hangover. He's the gentleman propped in the entrance of the public convenience just behind Paddington Tube Station. When I found him he seemed to have slumped disastrously into a twisted heap, the ragged corner of his raincoat floating on an ominous puddle. I straightened him out as best I could. He appeared to be dead – and to have been dead for some considerable time. There was no pulse at all, and his eye-balls had twisted around a full 180 degrees and were peering, if they saw anything at all, into the remains of his brain. However, every eighty-five seconds, on the second, a gas escaped from his slack jaw. (I hesitate to say mouth – for this had been turned into a toothless bearded gumhole, the size, significantly enough, of a wine cork.) I administered a few film cliches, like beating him about the face and neck, filling his rotting Australian bushranger's hat with water from the convenience and throwing it all over him, and once, perhaps twice, kicking him in the groin. The result was that every eighty-five seconds a whisper of ether escaped from his 'wine-hole'. Obviously a proper cure was needed.

With this in mind, I purchased from a nearby haberdashery an ugly little St Christopher's medal. I took it to the nearest gutter and stamped on it vigorously. At the newsagents I selected a postcard showing a colourful display of the Horseguards Parade, with Buckingham Palace prominent in the background. On this I wrote, with meticulous hand, the vital instructions. Being rather well-dressed at the time, I knew it was essential to find a somewhat shabby chemist. I had to scout around in the back streets for quite a while, knowing that time was running out – those little gasps were probably already stretching to ninety-five or one hundred second intervals. But I found just the shop: obviously fully stocked, but driven by economic necessity to display the odd article of medical hosiery, a vibro machine and a slim volume on the more mechanistic aspect of marital difficulties.

There was only one elderly man behind the counter, and to him I spoke openly and kindly:

'Good morning. I wonder if you would be good enough to give me a mixture containing five parts tetrahydrocannabinol acid, fifteen parts chloral-hydrate crystalline, Cardiaconal Adrenaline extract, suspended in one hundred parts surgical spirits.'

It was obvious, immediately, that never in his entire career of post-graduate pharmaceutical studies, nor in his vast experience as a prescribing chemist, had anyone ever attempted to mix these four ingredients, leave alone walk in off the street on a sunny morning and simply order them.

'I'm awfully sorry, sir', he stammered, 'but you'll need a prescription, two prescriptions, three . . . in fact I'm not all that sure . . .'

'Good Lord,' I interrupted, then went on: 'They didn't tell me that.'

'They, sir? Someone told you?'

'Yes. It's all rather difficult, isn't it? I was at the Imperial War Museum this morning, and they said . . . here, they wrote it down for me.' With this I reached into my breast pocket and carefully extracted the post card. I offered it to him, saying:

'Is that the stuff? Did they get it straight?'

The friendly chemist took the offered post card, duly noting the dashing Horseguards and the Royal architecture, then turning it over stared with quivering, hairy eyebrows. Eventually, without looking up, he said in a whispering voice that had become resigned and saddened to the complete degradation of all man and of all man's institutions:

'The Imperial War Museum.'

'Yes, indeed. I don't know what I shall do now. They had nothing down there that would help me. They suggested that I get some of that made up.'

The elderly man was still shaking his head. 'The Imperial War Museum,' he repeated. Then looking slowly up at me he went on:

'You were at the Imperial War Museum, sir? And they told you they had nothing which would help. Then they told you to get this made up?'

'That's it,' I agreed, 'and within the hour, they said.'

The man slowly ran the back of his hand across a bushy brow, then turned to gaze, as if for the last time, at the tools of his profession – the glass containers, crucibles, ointments.

'I'm an old man, sir, and there are a lot of things I don't

grasp as quickly as I used to. I would consider it a privilege, then, if you would tell me what circumstances led the Imperial War Museum to prescribe,' and he looked briefly at the card, 'five parts tetrahydrocannabinol acid, fifteen parts chloral-hydrate crystalline, Cardiaconal Adrenaline extract, suspended in one hundred parts surgical spirit.'

'Well, it's rather embarrassing.'

'I dare say, sir. I dare say. But life seems to be passing me by these days and the confusion of channging events . . .'

'This,' I told him, dramatically producing the twisted bit of tin, 'is the British Empire Silver Medal of Valour. It became obsolete just before the war. It's a strange medal – awarded under strange cricumstances. It was given, posthumously, of course, to the families of those men of the Secret Service, like my father, who, while on duty abroad . . . died . . . under circumstances too awful . . . without . . . who to the very end . . . never . . .'

The chemist's eyebrows, though he continued to stare at me, were drooping in awful understanding. The howls of tortured men disturbed his vision. Ignorant foreign thugs, with vile political schemes at hand, screwing the limbs off British men. In the damp cellers, below the hard naked bulbs – these men endured alone the sordid beatings, the bash of rifle butts, the sadism of thumb-screw operatives and the searing burns from cheap continental fags, praying for the ultimate mercy of the brick wall outside – and keeping the secret forever British. Then I let him have the crunch. I blurted:

'For those who died silent.'

With some reverence he took the trodden bit of dirty tin from my hand and held it in his. He looked at it for a while and spoke solemnly:

'And all they got was this – posthumously. Oh, it's a good medal I dare say, precious silver, craftsmanship and all that – but still . . . just a medal.'

'Well, actually, that's the bit that's rather embarrassing.

It seems that things generally were pretty rough in those years and these were not made from pure silver. Far from it, apparently. They're rotting, or whatever metal does. What with this, and being obsolete, and never recognised in the first place, there's a small investiture at the Palace today. Re-investiture, I suppose. I wanted to hand father's back in good condition. Hence the Imperial War Museum, where they said they could do nothing in so short a time and suggested five parts you know what.'

All was restored in the old chemist's faith. He nodded several times at the ironies of life – but he was visibly relieved that honour somehow continued to be given where honour was due.

'I'll make up a bottle of it,' he smiled, taking the card with him behind a further counter. He rooted round for an empty bottle, a cork that would fit, and the various ingredients. He spoke to me as he worked:

'Admittedly I don't have a degree in metalurgy, and I don't know what the medal's made of, but I'd sure as hell like to know what it is you clean with the active ingredient of cannabis, plus one of the world's most universal sedatives mixed with heart stimulant and added to ninety-eight percent pure alcohol!'

Before giving me the bottle, the good chemist set about labelling it from a collection of stickers below the counter. The first to go on was NOT TO BE TAKEN and under this he adjusted DRUGS. From somewhere he found POISON and also a three large XXX s. Not content, he added a large label KEEP OUT OF CHILDREN'S REACH and a smaller warning KEEP AWAY FROM FIRE. These were quickly followed by THIS PRESCRIPTION CANNOT BE REPEATED WITHOUT A FURTHER NOTE FROM YOUR DOCTOR and a brilliantly red DANGER, and, from somewhere, a blue AIR MAIL.

'I would strongly advise, sir, that when you've finished with this, you do not throw it down the sink or flush it away. I don't like the idea of it entering the public water system in any form. No, I should be inclined to burn it. Stand as far back as you can from a bonfire in an open field and throw it in . . . and remember to run, won't you, sir?'

It was sometime before I managed to find our gentleman of the sorrows. Frankly, I wasn't too keen to be close to him again, and the thought of it put me in need of one or two cures myself. In fact, my return to him was in the order of an 'appointment'; and one of the characteristics of the hangover which I have discovered is that any form of appointment, work, or mental exercise, leads to a healthy intake of alcohol, sometimes to the sensible point of cancelling those matters.

When I did return to the public convenience the bush-ranging gentleman was no longer alone. Pawing through his pockets was a smallish animal dressed entirely in black. This felon stopped as I approached. He looked straight at me, somehow knowing that we were both interested in the same body.

'What d'you want, mister?' he asked with a thoroughly evil smile. After a moment I replied:

'I've come to give him a drink. I think he needs it.'

'We all need a drink, don't we?'

'Well, you can run along and get your own. I have something rather special for this gentleman.'

'He's full of it, mister. Smells like Brasso. Anyway, give the stuff to me. He's dead.'

For some reason I was quite shocked by this.

'Dead!' I said. 'Can't be dead. I need him.'

By pinching the gentleman's cheeks I managed to get his cork hole open. The weed beside me gasped as I produced my explosive bottle.

'Here, give us some of that, mister. Wasted on him. I need it. Need it so . . .'

'Shut up, you insect's turd found in your mother's hairy ass.' Well, I was upset, and strongly concerned for the old gentleman.

When I poured the fluid down the wine-hole nothing

happened. It spilled a bit, but most of it simply lay stagnating in his chops. Artificial respiration was just not on. Instead I closed his jaws and rattled his head. When I again peered in through the little hole it was gone. I repeated the process. Press jowls. Hole opens. Pour in fluid. Close mandibles. Rattle head. Open up – all gone.

I do wish, Professor, I had some command of words. It would make my lot in this Asylum a pleasant one indeed were there only some way of conveying to you the profundity and the joy of what took place. We have all paid the unnecessary price of wholesome living, we have all known that the end was at hand. It is unlikely, however, that we will ever experience such a cure for such a hangover as this Paddington cadaver. Due no doubt to the shape of his mouth, there escaped from his shocked lungs a distinct low whistle. It was, I now believe, the breath of life. His frame jerked and the eyes flew open, flaring agoggle at the world he had not yet left. Then he saw me clearly, and the bottle in my hand, and he understood. He didn't exactly smile – not with that mouth – but I'm sure his eyes did melt somewhat. He spoke to me.

'God bless you, son.'

'Here,' snarled the lout. 'What you want from him, then? Why'd you give the old fool that stuff. Said you wanted something.'

Without a shake or a tremor, the gentleman gently took the bottle from my hand and, adjusting it so that the opening of the bottle was firmly screwed into the receiving lip hole, he tilted his head back. A mouthful of fluid guggled down. He brought his head forward and unscrewed the bottle from his mouth. Immediately, all human life passed behind his eyes.

'You wanted something, son?'

'Yes, yes, I did rather.'

'What can I do for you?'

'Well, actually,' I said, 'I really wanted to get your views on hangovers. I'm trying to find out about them, and I thought you might know.'

'Hangovers,' the man repeated, and was obviously thinking.

I don't know what I expected, Professor. I knew he was not going to mess about with any desciptions. I hoped rather, that he might utter some such sagacious pearl as 'Life is a hangover' or 'I am a hangover' but I'm afraid humanity had stepped beyond the discipline of science – the man was over-cured. He told me:

'Hangovers? I don't think I can remember one. Might have had 'em, of course, but damned if I can remember one.'

With this he quietly finished the bottle; and, knowing that he was now at peace and could require nothing further from me, I moved off. At the corner I looked back. I will never know why the scene seemed so charged with significance or why it should remain with me always. The gentleman was slumped comfortably on his back, with the Australian bushrangers hat askew on his head. One arm was stretched along the ground, and the other lay on his stomach, holding the empty bottle. Beside him crouched the black insect, unable to understand what his eyes had just witnessed.

Oh, my God, I have perceived the mysteries of Your ways and I know that You liveth. I have seen You strike down the ignorant and lay waste . . .

Yes, well. Here Kent's temporary illness seems to be getting the better of him and we might leave it at that.

What we must do though, is face this horrid problem of the hangover. Many critics of Asmolianism claim that it is the nemesis of our system, while faint hearts look upon it as some form of defeat. I assure you it is neither. We would surely have been stopped very early in our studies if we had not overcome this problem.

Right from the start we had to put in a great deal of urgent work here. Not only did the students have hangovers in the normal course of events, they had to acquire them to study them. Our psychological tests on sufferers showed an acute obsession with time. Without exception, everyone tested wanted time to pass at a rate quite different from the norm. Eighty-five per cent answered 'No' to question 14*a*:

14*a*: Do you wish you were still asleep?
Yes: 15% No: 85%
14*b*: If not, why not?
95% answered to the effect that they would only have to wake up again.

You will notice the subtle concern with time: few wanted to go back in time because they would not like to come forward again. (The missing 5% in 14*b* will prove most significant.)

Again, in question 372, we find much the same pattern.

372*a*: Would you like to take off your wrist watch?
Yes: 75% No: 10% Don't know: 15%
372*b*: If so, why so?
60% said they wanted to get rid of the noise; a significant 30% answered that they did not want to look at the time any more.

It's rather obvious, is it not, that what is appearing here is a pattern of acute repugnance with the present time. (The missing 10% in 372*b* by the way, replied that they wanted their wrist watches removed to enable them to lift their left arms while the missing 5% in 14*b* were unable to see, read, understand or answer the question).

You will no doubt remember Kent's remarks from the field – that time future must remain clear of obstacles. We also know from our work at the Institute that the *subjective* time values of any person are distorted when hungover: naturally, on the principle of Pinnoccio's nose, all is relative. However, time judgments seemed to be grossly altered. We have kept some sufferers away from clocks and watches, asking them, exactly every half hour, to judge the time. Perhaps it is not surprising that they were all hopelessly wrong – we must bear in mind their condition. What is significant here is that not one of them realised that he was being asked every half hour.

All of them, without exception, were of the opinion that the timing was haphazard and that the intervals varied from ten minutes to – in one incubus sufferer – three and a half hours.

We also have the evidence of reversed time for the two types of Asmolian – the natural five per cent alcolergics and the ninety-five per cent who have acquired the mastery through intelligent and guided practice.

Therefore, I would like now to pass on our advice, not to say system, for dealing with hangovers. But as this is one of the areas where the two types of Asmolian seem to differ (in that time, as a healer, is reversed for the alcolergic) I would like to refer to a medical specialist – a practice, as you may have already observed, I abhor and avoid.

I mentioned the alcolergic as one fortunate to carry the Asmol blueprint in his system, much like a film that simply needs developing. This blueprint, like the DNA molecular structure, is carried in the nervous system and reacts with the blood chemistry under appropriate stimuli.

We are not alone in this particular discovery, though we are the only people in this field to view alcolergy in perspective – as a natural prototype to be emulated. Working along similar lines, but to utterly opposed ends, the American biochemist, Dr Freile Fleetwood, has described this phenomenon in what he likes to call the 'alcoholic'. Rather simplisticly, he refers to 'substances' in the blood which vary according to moods. Intense moods such as anxiety, tension and resentment can produce a marked increase in these substances. The alcolergic (or 'alcoholic' as he prefers to call such prodigies) reacting to such intense moods, produces a unique and distinctive species of these substances – a species which is negated or destroyed by alcohol. Thus the alcolergic is in the happy position of being married biochemically to alcohol. What a very, very convenient marriage.

I would like to quote to you now from the works of Dr Lindoln Williams, an astute writer whose aims, most unfortunately, are as misguided as those of Dr Fleetwood – as will be obvious by his use of such words as 'alcoholism' 'problem' and 'suffer'. Writing in 1960, of Dr Fleetwood's findings, he states:

> According to Fleetwood's experiments, six ounces of whisky abolish or nearly abolish the tension and resentment substances in the alcoholic, but modify them only slightly in the non-alcoholic. This would suggest that moderate drinkers, whose intake over a period of years may run into barrelfuls without seeming to do any harm, are free from this biochemical idiosyncrasy. If this theory is sound then the notion that alcoholism is solely derived from the consumption of alcohol is a misconception. The source of the problem is the user of the alcohol and not the alcohol itself.
>
> Fleetwood's investigations are still proceeding and no final conclusions can yet be drawn from them, but no other research seems to have come so close to the discovery of a chemical idiosyncrasy in the bodies of those who suffer from alcoholism.

WELL IT HAS NOW, SIR!

But to continue. The cure for all hangovers and all their symptoms, regardless of whether one feels that time will make them slightly better or infinitely worse, is profoundly and majestically simple.

First, the root of the word intoxication is, strangely enough, toxic. When one is toxic, feeling lethargic and irritable, there is nothing like a stiff drink to get things sorted out.

Secondly, the metabolic activity needed during the night to get rid of the alcohol can result in very real exhaustion. There is only one universal remedy for temporary exhaustion, and that is a stiff drink.

Thirdly, the consumption of alcohol on the previous evening may well have resulted in irritation and inflammation of the gastro-intestinal tract. Now, we all know how to deal with the grippy tummy – that's right, a stiff drink. And surely it is not necessary to advise on the remedy for the severe dehydration caused by alcohol!

As for the more general aches and pains, what is needed is a temporary anaesthetic. There is no greater anodyne on this earth than a stiff drink.

For the alcolergic's unique problem, the interim, wherein he feels, and correctly feels, that time will only make things worse and bring on withdrawal symptoms, logic tells us to shorten the interim and avoid withdrawal. Again, and finally, a stiff drink – and what one stiff drink can do, two can do better. In fact, inescapable logic leads us through the day's first bottle and well into the land of the living.

We would be very proud indeed at the Institute if we could say that we had discovered the universal cure for the hangover. As you can well imagine, we tried hard to improve on what is already in existence. We have come to the happy and humble conclusion that it cannot be done.

Aside from getting booze into the system as soon as possible, there are one or two aids which we have discovered at the Institute to be most ameliorative. And so I would like to end my talk to you today by giving you some of the practicable results of our experiments. I think it is the first time in this series of lectures that I have been able to pass on the concrete results of our work. So here, straight from the Institute, you might say, are a few *do's* and *don'ts*.

Don't have a bath. It seems a good idea, doesn't it? You hear people tell how they got into a good hot bath and soaked it all out. Well, whatever else they may have done, they did not cure themselves. Our tests show that baths are extremely enervating, and easily sap what little energy is left in a hungover body. This invariably leads to a weak form of nervous trembling, as if one had already taken one's last breath – some time ago. Our tests show a marked drop in blood pressure, which is hardly ideal when there is already a distinct sensation of having bled to death during the night.

Do have sex – if at all possible. Minute examination of some of our workers' uterine membrane revealed indications of irritation, caused, we feel, by the alcohol in the tissue. It would hardly be in keeping with the Asmolian philosophy for anyone to deny themselves the pleasure of scratching an itch. Neural tests at the Institute show that an orgasm quietens the nerves somewhat, and for this reason is certainly to be desired.

There is one danger here; with the irritation of uterine membrane, orgasm should be achieved almost immediately. If this does not occur, then STOP. Climax will not be achieved for ages, by which time one's limited store of energy has long been exhausted. Most of our people feel that, to avoid embarrassment or inadvertent insult, this should somehow be made clear at the outset. Use some phrase which, with some subtlety and delicacy, tastefully explains your position. Our standard sentence, with personal variations as you wish, can be used by either partner:

'Look, I want a screw, and if you don't make me come immediately I'm off to the boozer.'

Most people understand quite clearly what's on your mind.

Don't smoke. For God's sake, whatever you do, don't smoke.

Do gawk, if you feel it's there. This may seem strange – why should anyone swing over the lavatory spewing up his heart? Well, frankly, if it's there, it's better out. Also, there is the fear – a justified fear once one is in the pub – that it could come up at quite the wrong time. And we did finally find out why it is that drinkers don't really mind the gawks, no matter how horrible they are. This is so, basically, because of the sense of helplessness experienced by the sufferer – there seems nothing he can do. With the gawks, however, he feels he is making some progress, something is at least happening, and if this vile fluid is rejected by the body, surely the body will recover more quickly. All this is highly suspect, but we do not frown upon auto-suggestion. We are certainly in favour of anything that helps to avoid the problem of Dermot Brine.

On one particularly bad morning at the local pub,

it took an hour and a half and nine lost large gins to keep the first one down. A good gawk would have saved him the best part of five quid. Certainly there is no need for his present carry-on. He comes into the Bells, at about noon, when the place is beginning to fill. He stands rigidly at the bar for some time, his face changing colour slowly but vividly – similar to a chameleon staring at a rainbow. When the barmaid asks him what he wants he replies in a raspy but clearly audible voice:

'Gin and two fish hooks, please.'

Don't make any appointments whatsoever; cancel those you have and confine your social activities to the 'group'. This syndrome of time and approaching appointments is known as 'Kent's Hysteria'. The major symptom with this problem is that the closer one gets to the appointed hour, regardless of cures, the more noticeable becomes the shaking peripheral neuritis. Kent's Hysteria is not helped by the knowledge that even though vast intakes of alcohol can temporarily stop the sweats, there is no assurance that this anaesthetic may not wear off rapidly during some important meeting. The idea of arriving at the bank, full of dash and confidence, only to watch the manager surveying you ever more suspiciously – as you suddenly get the ab-dabs and gasp – is just not on. Better to cancel the appointment.

Do admit to a hangover to any and all who feign interest. It does, after all, show that you are living life fully. In any case, there is no known successful way of concealing the fact. *One simply cannot watch every limb at the same time* – and why the hell should one? Always remember that if for any reason you feel uncomfortable discussing your hangoever, then you are in the wrong company. Leave it immediately and head for group therapy with your own people.

Don't sign anything. You're likely sign *any*thing. Besides, it's quite impossible to explain away 'Not Usual Signature' on a cheque which was written at ten o'clock in the morning.

Don't drink coffee, whatever you do. There are endless cartoons showing the head of the family sitting at the breakfast table with ice packs on dome, coffee in hand. Whoever draws these vicious jokes most certainly does not drink at all. It's a sedative one needs, not a stimulant. Even worse, coffee plays hell with the nervous system. During the night alcohol has attacked the fatty tissue which normally protects our nerves – they are now *exposed*. What is needed is a good chew at your tranquilisers. Valium and Librium are excellent – phenobarbitone is best. Tryptophen Forte is handy if you're not used to it, likewise Largactil and Lithium. And a Mandrax or Mogadon will solve even the most recalcitrant problem for at least an hour.

Do avoid the following claustrophic situations: public transport of any kind – you are in the hands of others; air travel, for the same reason – but much worse; traffic jams, theatres, cinemas, crowds, construction sites, kindergartens, record shops and fun fairs. Never, under any circumstances, join a queue.

Leaving you with these practical results of some of our work, and having explained the hangover and its cure, I hope this tiresome obstacle to a fuller existence has been removed from your minds and that you are now able to embark on the road to the riotous life we all so richly deserve.

Five First Signs of Hope

Ladies and Gentlemen: Since speaking to you last I have been attacked by the press. The snide references in the newspapers, in regard to Eamonn Kelly particularly, are nothing new to me. It is another matter, however, when, as a result of these lectures, an Outside Broadcasting Unit enters the grounds of the Asmolian Institute and aims one of its cameras through the window of our Cocktail Bar. Their pictures and their film, taken out of context and introduced with appropriate heavy sarcasm, might indeed have made good television. Fortunately, these films will never be seen by the general public. The television camera will never be used again, and the six members of the crew may be seen at the Hammersmith General Hospital during normal visiting hours – except for the gentleman with the torn pectoral muscles, who may be out of Casualty at any time within the next year or so. No doubt these men are, or were, very clever at their craft, but they overlooked two things – our male nurses, Looey and Bluey.

Let me again make this one point perfectly clear: I have every intention, probably during this talk today, of explaining fully what happened to Eamonn Kelly. Mr Kelly is, or was (no, still *is*, in a way) a researcher working for the Asmolian Institute. His experiences and the findings of his colleagues constitute important contributions to science. But let me also make another point clear: it is grossly misleading (and, on the part of a lecturer, irresponsible) simply to rattle off a case history without at the same time ensuring that these facts will be understood. Kelly must be seen in context.

Kelly is a pure Asmolian, an alcolergic; and he came to us an already highly developed alcolergic. It will be understood, therefore, that from time to time it became necessary to restrain Eamonn, both in the interests of scientific research and his own well being. Now one could hardly expect even our Chief Nurse, Agatha Huntington, to attempt the restraint of a boozed-up ranting Paddy. Clearly male nurses were called for. Also, at about this time, the press were becoming interested in us. Obviously unable to find the news, leave alone print it, they resorted to their usual practice of fabricating it, using as a basis for this fiction some person or event known to the public. For some reason beyond my knowledge of media, the Asmolian Institute forms such a platform and on it they erected some fanciful myths indeed. Other papers and magazines followed suit. Being no-news we became big news. Even a cursory search of the grounds at that time would reveal men of Current Affairs, women from magazines, Swedish sociologists and interviewers in depth. Something had to be done.

I discussed this problem with my now considerable staff and it was Hamilton Hamilton who came up with the answer.

'We need male nurses, Professor,' he said to me as we were taking sherry in my office. 'And we also need public relations men to deal with the newsmen in the garden. Someone to beat the shit out of them.'

'There's a great deal in what you say, Ham,' I replied, looking out of the window where I could see a photographer too drunk to focus either his eyes or his contraption. 'Public relations, eh? How many do you think it would take to kick the cobblers off those coyotes?'

'An army, if you picked the wrong sort,' Hamilton answered. 'But choose the right men and you need only a few. Remember Kenya, the Congo, French Canada? Just a few mercenary bastards and your problem's gone.'

'Agreed, Hamy, agreed. Yet I don't quite see Mad Mike Hoare as a male nurse, though Eamonn's behaviour when sloshed . . .'

'I can probably arrange something there,' Hamilton offered. 'I was never a socialite, you know, but I moved in high society.

Therefore I was associating with mugs, thugs and corruption. I'll drop into the "Aimer's" and see what I can find.'

'The "Aimer's," Ham? The "Aimer's"? Tell me immediately.'

'It's a London club. Well patronised by the theatre crowd, politicians and the underworld. The two men who throw you out there don't just bounce you – they *aim* you. Their names are Looey and Bluey.'

'But if they're already employed, Ham, they're hardly available right now.'

'They're always employed and always available. I wouldn't say they'd serve two masters – their combined brains wouldn't rise to it – but money will move them anywhere.'

When Looey and Bluey came for their interview they stood at my desk like a pair of uncomfortable automatons. It was difficult to tell them apart; and though they no doubt have other distinguishing characteristics, I find it easiest to remember that Looey has no left ear and Bluey is the one who, during what must have been a harrowing fracas, had his nose bitten off.

'Gentlemen, I can see that we're more or less agreed about your duties. The last point to discuss, it seems, is remuneration.'

'Well, Boss,' Bluey said nasally (if one without a nose can be so described), 'down at the Club we get fifty nicker each. That's for the whole week, see. Fifty nicker each, like. A ton the pair.'

'Rather steep, isn't it?' I queried uselessly. 'I suppose, then, we'll have to run to a hundred and twenty five.'

'But, Chief,' replied Looey (and those of you who have seen the film "2001" will remember the computer's voice as it ran out of steam), 'what we got to think of is our reputate . . . reputepute . . . our reprep . . . what people is saying. I mean to say if they was saying we was shifty like just for the bread.'

'An admirable regard for one's standing in any profession is no bad thing. At the same time, I think a hundred and fifty would be our limit.'

Hamilton at this moment coughed, twice. It is presumably some form of code used by the stupifyingly wealthy to indicate to the craven indigent that they have got all they are going to get. It irked me at the time, but the two zombie garrotters agreed:

'You're all right, Captain.'

'That's what he says, Master.'

So all seemed settled; though there was still one point worrying some part of my mind. It was not exactly a thought: more a group of thought patterns. These men could be bought . . . at the right price . . . say two hundred a week . . . those walking knackers could turn on anyone . . . me . . . Hamilton . . . the staff . . . and some arcanum between Hamy and themselves.

'There's just one point, gentlemen,' I said as I slid open the bottom drawer of my desk. 'Something of a test, you might say. The packet of money which I am placing before you contains exactly five hundred pounds. It is kept in my drawer for emergencies, and I shall be expecting you to protect it in future. But for the moment I would like you to touch it and feel it. Let the wad rest heavy in your hand, Looey. That's it. Feels nice, does it not? A right little bundle, wouldn't you say? Now let Bluey handle it. Well done, Bluey, but no grabbing now. No, Bluey! No, you're not to eat it! Put it down on the desk. There's a good chap.'

The men were narcosed. All movement was liquid and the river of being had borne away all anxiety. Everything was certainty now.

'You are naturally affable men, both of you. You will always be firm but most gentle with the patients, even a Mr Eamonn Kelly. Should there be intruders, as there are now, I would expect you to deal with them in your own way, whatever that might be. And naturally both these tasks will be considered your normal duties. But there will be special occasions . . . special assignments, you might call them. Something over and above your normal duties. I'm not naive, gentlemen. I know that a contract includes certain contingencies and excludes others. Some extra financial arrangement will have to be made as and when these occasions arise. Do I make myself clear.'

'Five by five.'

'Right down the line, Champ.'

'Well, one of those occasions exists at the moment. There is a special person I would like you to beat up. To bash. How much from the kitty on the desk there.'

'Is it a Constitutional job?' asked the cretin who could pronounce such words.

'Constitutional?'

'Yeah, is he in or out.'

I looked to Hamilton. Communications seemed to have broken down utterly. But Hamy was as relaxed as ever and gave a simple translation:

'Front Bench or Shadow Cabinet?'

'Good Lord, no!' I assured them. 'Just someone you wouldn't like to beat up. Say your previous employer, for instance. I want to test you. To see if you really will carry out my orders – regardless.'

'Want a week's screw for that, Commander.'

'Yeah, a ton and a half for a turnover like that.'

'Splendid.'

I did not hurry overmuch as I counted out to each of them the seventy five stiff articles of corruption. When they had the money well stuffed into their pockets I gave them their simple orders.

'I would like you to beat up Mr Hamilton Hamilton.'

It was the first occasion on which I had ever seen Ham really badly rattled. He fully realised his impossible position and was on his feet immediately.

'Hold it, Looey! Bluey, for Christ's sake, it's me! Old Ham! I'm telling you. Don't do it. Get away, you oafs. Well fuck you, Asmol. Aaah. Fuck you to hell. Stop it. It's my money you're paying them with. Looey, that's an arm lock! Ooooh! I've got more money. I'm rich. Stinking . . . aaach. Bluey, don't aim like that! Money, money, I've lots of . . . aaaaaaaaaaaagh!'

I had to put a stop to it, of course. Hamilton seemed already to be broken in several places. He fell into the corner, gasping – searching, it seemed, for his tongue.

'Now, gentlemen, while the adrenal flows, while you're in the mood, as you might say, come with me to the window.'

I drew the curtains and several faces peered in.

'That's him,' shouted one fool.

'Who are the machines?' asked another.

'Hey, someone's passed out in the corner. Look at him!'

I let Looey and Bluey gaze for some time at this mob and at the dozens milling about. Then I smiled at the two high-binders and said:

'I would like to see these people elsewhere.'

Looey and Bluey just looked at me! They obviously wanted to help but couldn't. Something had gone wrong, something I could not be aware of. Hamilton groaned from the floor:

'They don't understand you.'

With relief I returned my eyes to the murder-machines and pointed to the window:

'Throw every fuck-face off the grounds!'

What a sight! The first half dozen or so actually tried to interview Bluey. One man could be seen being force-fed with his camera. The Fourth Estate was in disarray and panic swept through their ranks as they fled to any and all possible exits, spurred to greater speed by the sound of their colleagues' crunching bones. Looey found one crafty correspondent trying to cilmb a willow tree and assisted him in a most direct and forceful manner.

Oh, my God, I have perceived the mysteries of Your ways and I know that You liveth. I have seen You strike down the ignorant and lay waste to the corrupted lands of Your Principality.

*

Now let us clarify this whole business of Eamonn Kelly. Eamonn is a natural Asmolian, and due to our good work now lives, permanently, deep in the fantastic world of Korsakoff's Syndrome. Now Korsakoff's Syndrome (or Psychosis, if you want to be as nasty as the doctors) is indicated by one very simple but hugely effective symptom – no memory. I do not mean impairment of memory or the inability to remember certain facts, nor even the difficulty of remembering what happened at the party on the previous evening. I refer to a mind from which, due to alcoholic intake, the memory box has mercifully been fused – permanently.

As you can well imagine, the rest of the mind finds this state rather peculiar; it has always used memory – instant memory – as an integral part of thought. Thus, when such a computer needs memory in order to function, and finds that there is none available, then a memory is instantly manufactured, or *confabulated*, in order to allow the thought pattern to continue. When the thought pattern has been fulfilled, the manufactured memory is no longer required and is returned to the memory box – but in this case simply disappears into a void.

On high mountains the world over you will find peaceful men of recluse; in monasteries you will find them praying; in temples you will find their bodies twisted in yoga and in the bushes of Tanganyika they can be found driving wooden stakes into each other's foreheads. 'What are they doing?' you may well ask. In their different ways they are trying to achieve that state in which Kelly lives – Nirvana.

For us, Eamonn Kelly is the Guru, the Sufi. He is the one who has not only been there, but is still there. We mortals use alcohol and the Asmolian system so that we may glimpse at the infinite. Eamonn no longer needs the stimulant or the discipline – he lives there.

And how did he get there? Quite simply, from 'Nirvana Minus'. 'Nirvana Minus' is a condition reached after one has done everything that possibly can be done. The patient has completed the Asmolian course and waits, limbo-like, to move forward into permanent peace. People in Nirvana Minus are to be respected and perhaps, in anticipation, revered. They have cast off the shackles of employment, discarded the vanity of fashion and have come to realise that the only moral source of income is from freely given alms. Like Bartholomew Kent's gentleman at the Paddington convenience, they have escaped the sordidity of our modern world. And for this unpardonable breach in our mumbo-jumbo ant heap, society takes its revenge by calling them unemployable drunkards reduced to rags and begging. Yet urban man is not unaware of his profanity and, with final irony, has named a street after the men he has murdered – Skid Row.

Naturally, we at the Institute cannot claim any honours for the whole of Kelly's progress from mediocrity to Korsakoff; though we were directly responsible for the last great push. As I've said, Kelly came to us a natural alcolergic Asmolian. Furthermore, he was well advanced in the discipline. It is as a result of our subsequent studies that we realise this now; at the time we were still formulating our basic theories. Thus, in order to fully understand that state in which Eamonn Kelly now exists, it would be helpful if I were to show you the path he must have followed – if almost instantaneously. It is a trail along which we must all go a-winding.

The path to Nirvana Minus is chartered through three very distinct areas. Each area represents a process of learning. We are involved firstly with the personality, then with the mind and lastly with the body. These three areas are referred to thus:

1. *Discovery – by the personality*
2. *Confirmation – the mind adjusts*
3. *Release – the body concurs*

Many of you will want to know immediately what area you're in and how far you've progressed. A number of you will wonder whether or not you have even started, while others will query whether all the good work they have put in is showing satisfactory results. All this is very natural and shows a healthy interest in one's progress. With this in mind, I'd like to familiarise you with some of the findings of the Institute in this particular regard. Bear in mind at all times the three stages to which I have just referred: I will assume that you are doing so and will try not to be repetitive about these points. Remember, too, that it is not necessary to exhibit any number of these hopeful signs: just one will do. You're on the right road.

THE SILENT CONTRACT

Any pact with oneself to somehow control the intake of alcohol.

Though supposedly silent, these treacherous treaties are invariably sprayed at friends, relatives, spouses, colleagues, and, with tortuous and devious subtlety, employers. Regardless of whether they remain silent or are published on the back page of *The New York Times*, all such promises are the same in one respect – they will be broken.

This is so for the very good reason that they are impossible to keep and would not have been made in the first place if they were possible. By their very creation they bring one to the borders of lunacy.

'I'm going to watch my drinking in future.'

Just what is meant by this classic campaign is now beyond the best minds working in Etymology today. Is one to understand that the utterer of this promissory impossibility intends to stare at himself in the bar room mirror until he slips noiselessly to the floor? Has he a photographic device as a visual aid in recalling that explosive moment when he walked through the front room window in answer to the door bell? Or has he, do you think, every intention of arriving at the Chancellor's dinner party with the bathroom mirror secreted in his cummerbund, somehow hoping to float it on his soup as he scoffs the hooch?

And such contracts as 'First sherry when the kids are in bed' can lead to situations as that reported from Uville, Kentucky, where, so the court was told, a strapping great youth of sixteen was being sent to bed, complete in his American football clobber, at three o'clock in the afternoon.

No – we must ask ourselves what is happening here? A person whose drinking habits were such that alcohol was a matter of indifference is now entering into committed contracts concerning the stuff. And what has happened here is quite simple – discovery. The personality has discovered that alcohol can free one from the vicious bonds of society.

What has also happened here – and we will now be greatly concerned with this for the duration of these lectures – is that society, to guard itself, has exerted moral pressure on the individual personality. No society could continue to exist, to cohese, if a sizeable number of its members were to enjoy individuality to the point of Asmolianism. The United States of America, a thorough nation if nothing else, went so far, in trying to protect itself, as to ennact Prohibition. We know that this had no effect whatsoever on dedicated Asmolians, though it did manage to corrupt for all time the intsitutions of law, order, democracy and education.

If such a fear exists, you may ask, then why don't we know about it? We're afraid of Communism and we talk about it. We abhor Civil War, but we have lots of words with which to discuss it – riots, civil disobedience, special power's acts, etc. Where's this great fear of the free Asmolian? Precisely where you found the other two fears – in our words.

Drunken Bastard, is a good one. *Drunk and Disorderly* is used wherever English is spoken. And here are a few more. Notice how readily they register on the conditioned mind:

Pissed, gassed, stupefied, arsehoes, stewed, corned, besotted, beered, befuddled, thick, tipsy, supped, bowled, blind, jagged, looped, jarred, torn, liquored, debauched, dipso, grogged, tight, boozed, soaked, pickled, three sheets in the wind, ginned up, squiffed, lushed, langers, magotty, sozzled, stoned, soused, bombed, oiled, stiff, boïled, canned, blotto, maudlin, bottled, pie-eyed, high, sodden, wino, guzzled, smashed and stinking rotten drunk.

Now then, Ladies and Gentlemen, though billions and billions of pounds are spent on the stuff, show me one complimentary phrase in that lot and I'll show you a society on the verge of disintegration.

*

THE SPECIAL OCCASION DRINK

When occasions call, not for a drink, but for two drinks.

It is not unnatural that man, when anticipating or participating in occasions of a special nature, should turn to that which is most beneficial to his soul. And there is indeed hope for you if you find yourself celebrating the good things of this life with alcohol. If our first sign of hope, the Silent Contract, was mainly concerned with stage one and the discovery of alcohol by the personality, then boozing it up on special occasions can certainly be said to fall into the category of stage two – confirmation by an adjustment of the mind.

You've just received a fat salary raise. This is wonderful! It represents added pleasure to your life, increased amenities and a future free of material anxiety. You should rush straight home to your wife and hug her. And an extra hug for the kiddies too, for their childhood will now have an increased dimension. And your brother in Canada – phone him! And mother, what about that holiday?

If there is any hope for you at all, Sir, you will not do these things – certainly not all of them. You will instead, by following the sensible instructions of your mind, end up, one way or another, pig-eyed assholes. You will not arrive at work the next morning (if you do arrive) looking like the firm's superman on the way to the top, but rather like the senile janitor who has just been sacked for masturbating, non-stop, for 32 hours in the shop window.

This is as it should be; hangovers can be cured but dead living can only be terminated. Your mind is on the right track and you are moving forward in Asmolian progression. As you do progress you will find that more and more of life's occasions are, in fact, special occasions that call for drinks. After all, it is far from impossible that next week someone else in your firm will get a raise, or someone in another firm. During that same week three thousand and forty seven children will have been born in England, and though it is unlikely that any of them will be yours (but if one of them *is* yours, then for God's sake man . . .) one may well be the child of a relative, a friend, a colleague or a pen pal. There are over two thousand sporting events in which you may feel yourself to be personally involved; some politician, somewhere, will endanger our national security, the enocomy and our chances of survival; in your immediate vicinity two people and three and a half dogs will be involved in motor accidents; and anyway, every fourteenth week your morning train will arrive on time.

The following is the only sensible attitude to special occasion drinking:

Mr Kenwood, tired from being bullied in the office, steps off the train and slouches towards home. Things are not going well. On top of everything else, he has come to notice some changes in his wife. He feels that, though she is still in her early forties, she is somehow 'slackening off'. In the last few years he has seen her behaving strangely, oddly, at cocktail parties – as if she was really drunk. Her interest in fashion designing has waned and sometimes she even looks dowdy. It's as if she were letting herself go, slipping on the years. And she used to be so house proud!

He slips the key into the latch and pushes himself into the hallway. There stands Sue (actually it has changed to Susanna recently), her feet apart, one hand on the wall. She seems to be speaking:

'How did things go at the office, dear?'

'Oh, so-so.'

'Really! This calls for a drink!'

Another fine example of special occasion drinking took place in the Press Lounge of the Yankee Stadium in New York City. Mr Charles Heatherton, who has now specialised for us in this field of early indications, was party to the scene. He had just arrived in New York and was being entertained by two gentlemen of the Press, a Mr Hal Hanks and a Mr Buzz Mathorn. They had suggested that he join them in the Press Lounge at Yankee Stadium as they themselves were keen fans of baseball, though supporters of the opposing teams playing that day, the New York Giants and the New York Yankees. Mr Featherton thought this would be an excellent opportunity to learn something about this mysterious and advanced form of rounders and agreed readily, arranging to look for them either at the bar of the lounge or at the huge glass viewing-window on the far side of the room.

Though he did manage to get from his hotel to the Stadium without being mugged, drugged or solicited, he was necessarily late (he travelled by what is known as the subway) in arriving to find his hosts at the wall of glass looking out over the triangled green field.

'Hey, Charles!' shouted Hal Hanks from the huge window. 'Glad you got here. You're late, but hell, you couldn't have come at a better time.'

'That's right, Charles,' agreed Buzz Mathorn enthusiastically. 'Somehow Hal's crappy old Giants have crept into a lead of eight to six. But we'll soon have the bastards on their knees. In fact I've just ordered a drink to celebrate. What would you like? Old Grandad Bourbon? Canadian Club Rye? Hey, BARTENDER!'

'Just a Scotch, if you don't mind,' answered Charles Heatherton somewhat nervously. 'With a little ice if they have it.'

'Hey you, Bartender. Over here. That's an Old Grandad and a Canadian Club plus a Scotch on the rocks this . . . CHRIST! Was that a foul ball?'

'Foul ball?' murmured Mr Heatherton, wondering if by chance the Americans had invented yet another cocktail for concussion.

'That's what it was, all right,' explained Buzz Mathorn with glee. 'The guy with the bat's got to hit the ball *into* the field, not kill the spectators. He's in trouble, Charles. That pitcher's got him all sized up and everyone around here except Hal knows that this eight-six lead is going to be wiped out.'

'But he's hitting the ball,' Hal enunciated very carefully. 'He – is – hitting – the – goddamn – ball.'

At this point Mr Heatherton found the bartender pressing into his hand a yard of glass, the bottom half of which was full of Titanic ice cubes and brackish fluid.

'IT'S A HIT!' screamed Hal Hanks. 'He's going for first – and he's there!'

Charles Heatherton stared with intensity at the movements on the field. One of the three men standing like toy soldiers on his mother's croquet lawn had retrieved the ball and bulleted the thing to a man who appeared to be standing on a bag of sawdust.

'No second base for him,' scoffed Buzz Mathorn.

'Oh, no?' sneered Hal. 'And who do you think is coming in to bat?' By turning his head back he washed down the remainder of his Old Grandad. 'Big Black Bongo. That's who. And that calls for a drink. BARTENDER!'

Charles Heatherton also attempted to finish his drink in a hurry. This resulted in a monumental cube from the National Ice Storage Company dislodging itself from the ice-pack at the end of his glass, hurtling down the tube and crashing into his sinus.

'That's an Old Grandad, a Canadian Club and a Scotch on the rocks.'

True enough, out on the field, something netted in Central Africa was now standing at the plate, dressed in what seemed to be diminutive pyjamas, and swinging a tapered Hemlock log in the general direction of the pitcher.

'Now you're in for it,' growled Hal. 'He'll knock it out of the park.'

'Crap,' replied Buzz, as the St Lawrence Seaway ice-flow seemed to be breaking up somewhere near the bar. 'He might eat it, but he'll never hit it.'

In fact Big Black Bongo bunted: he stepped forward towards the ball and using the bat like a rolling pin simply pushed the ball on to the ground. Then, as several people scrambled about, he ran like hell for first base and the man who was there ran like hell for second.

'Christ!'

'Jesus!'

'BARTENDER! Make those doubles. The Coal Tar Ton just bunted!'

It was while the bartender was pressing these long drinks into the hands of the fans that someone on the far side of the lounge groaned with apprehension and disbelief:

'They're sending out Billy the Bunter.'

All eyes turned to the short wiry man who now approached the plate.

'Hold it just there, bartender,' said Buzz sternly. 'Is it really the Bunter? I mean, Bongo bunts and they send out another bunter? Then you just go right back to the bar and pour us all some more of this stuff ?– including that man who first spotted Billy.'

The pitcher was obviously phased by this manoeuvre. By pointing his finger in several directions, and spitting tobacco juice in all, he instructed his men in the field to close up around the dreaded bunter. Then he stood for some time staring hard at the head of this small man, obviously calculating how far he could get the ball to penetrate into his cranium. The drinks had arrived when the pitcher threw the ball viciously at the man's left ear. The man carefully stepped back, swung the bat firmly but with precision and the ball sailed slowly over the pitcher, over short-stop, over second base and landed gently on the grass.

The place was in uproar. At least four men rushed towards the stationary ball, while the man on second base swerved towards third, the one on first slid into second and the batter trotted on to first.

'Fuck me, the bases are loaded,' moaned Buzz Mathorn. 'I need a drink. BARTENDER!'

These drinks had arrived while the next batter approached the plate. But the room was instantly motionless, not an ice cube clinked. The man was limping, grotesquely.

'By God,' whispered Hal Hanks with awe and reverence. 'It's old "out-of-the-ball-park" Otis.'

'Bourbon,' stated Buzz Mathorn. 'If it's the last drink I ever have I'm drinking to that man. Christ, Charles, this is history. BARTENDER!'

It took some time for this willowy man to get himself organised at the plate. By using the bat for further support he rammed his legs, tripod-like, into the ground. Then he straightened up his frame and adjusted his hat. The fresh drinks had arrived as he turned and stared, one man to one man, at the fastest pitcher in the United States. Then the ball spat towards him.

It was only a click. For a full second no one could see where the ball had been hit – but they knew. There it was, sailing out over centre field, a man running suicidally towards the wall.

Then crunch, he hit the wall, crumpled to the ground and the ball soared out into some New York traffic jam.

'It's out of the park!' screamed forty-five thousand men.

The man on third jogged to the home plate; the man on second trotted to third and home to the plate; the wiry little fellow on first sped around second and third and was crying as he crossed the plate. Otis limped around the diamond to the cheers of a crowd totally out of control. The cheering and the shouting, they say, could be heard in Washington D.C. But above it all could be heard the cry that goes up the world over when history is made before your very eyes:

'B-A-R-T-E-N-D-E-R!!!'

*

REGULATION OF FUEL INTAKE

Any daily schedule which is pre-set for alcohol.

This is a sign of hope in which, should you be enjoying it, you can truly take heart. This hopeful harbinger falls into our third area, that in which the body concurs – release. It is, admittedly, only a first indication; true enough, you will have to travel far in this area to reach Nirvana – but you're doing all right.

What has taken place here is a phenomenon we at the Institute have called 'the switch' or 'Hooking in'. Your body, for far too many years, has been bored almost into decrepitude with a steady diet of food. Now it is learning that there is stronger tack on the market and is demanding, quite rightly, its daily intake. This is the switch in metabolism – from dreary food to rarified alcohol. For encouragement, keep an eye on your diet; you should find yourself eating less, with increasing irregularity, and drinking, regularly, a great deal more. Do remember, alcohol is a food.

If your metabolic machine has switched fuels, it is not unnatural that regular times be set aside for intake. The perfect or complete switch is from three square meals a day to three round bottles a day. But long before completion of this cycle, society, with its omniferous pressures, will have exerted its checks. You are not yet ready for the full release of the Dawn Patrol or the straightforward and overt activities of Jules Clarron and Sir Alexander Saunders. They have broken the social rules; you will continue to work within them. And this brings us immediately to what is rapidly becoming one of the most important social activities of your day – lunch.

This is indeed a major re-fuelling stage. After all, your body has exhausted the supply you put in last night. During your sleep certain malicious organs have been breaking down and excreting your reserves. (Organs which nature, in her justified annoyance, will soon strike down with cirrhosis and cancer, pleurisy and peritonitis.) As you head for lunch (an increasingly early lunch) you are exhausted. You're not at your best, are you? In fact you feel a little flighty. And where does your body and your mind take you? To the lavatory? To the dining room? To the foyer? Hell no, it's *fuel* you need. You march straight to the bar. And it is here that you meet your friends and colleagues and luncheon guests; for they too have marched straight to the bar. They are all meeting at what can only be described as a major filling station.

If you found yourself at the bar for any other reason, it would not be surprising if you were to order a light beer, a shandy. After all, it is the first drink of the day. But that is entirely the point – so it's Bloody Marys, gins and tonics, Scotch and sodas, and an encyclopaedia of American cocktails too beautiful to name or describe. There isn't time to be messing about with lagers, light ales or long fizzy glasses of nonsense. Bang in the hard stuff – the system has run dry!

At the Institute one of our economic advisers raised the question of pre-lunch drinks – re-fuelling – and the national economy. He pointed out that he was unable to find any other product bought in such numbers by so many people in such a short time. He drew for our minds the picture of Any Street, Any City, at the beginning of the lunch hours: a street full of men and women in a great hurry, travelling most by foot to the nearest appointed watering hole, there to press close to the well and scoop in the juice. He asked us to contemplate the amount of money involved and to try to estimate the turnover in hard cash – and all for the same specific purpose.

We did try. We set up an Estimates Committee with sub-Committees for the procuring of information and evaluation. Out went thousands of questionnaires to pubs, restaurants and hotels. By this time the Institute had very firm connections in the United States and from here too we gained much information. Our American colleagues were of the opinion that they should restrict their survey to the Eastern Seaboard of America. This area gave them the necessary density in population along with a similarity in occupation and social habits.

In both countries, but in England particularly, we had to deal with differences in drinking patterns due to social ratification. For example, we accepted a figure of 80% of all gin and tonics to have been consumed for re-fuelling purposes; for the pint before lunch we could accept only a figure of 70%. We felt that a number of lunch-time drinks in hotels must be discounted as having been purchased by overseas visitors with a different time rhythm. Sherry was a difficult problem; sex is not a discriminatory barrier in Asmolianism, but we did have to consider that some such drinks were accepted only out of politeness. It was a lot of work and consumed a great deal of time, but I'm sure you'll agree that the figures justify our claims and vindicate our theories. In Great Britain, the amount of money spent on re-fuelling purposes at lunch time on any given working day amounts to £1.74 million. On the Eastern Seaboard the comparable figure is 10 million U.S. dollars.

This brings us directly to the pleasant subject of 'the group'. There has already been one reference to this, in my last lecture, and perhaps at the time you wondered what I meant. Well, it was Bartholomew Kent who put us on the right road. During his incarceration he was subjected to a particularly nasty form of medical anti-Asmolianism known as group therapy. Here a number of people who are dying for a drink are rounded up and closeted together with the purpose of talkin geach other out of it. It is rarely successful; in fact we have instances in America of entire groups disgorging themselves from Clinics and marching into the nearest bar, there to set about things in no uncertain fashion. There is no prettier sight to the inn-keeper than thirty or forty hardened drinkers, dry as bones, dashing from the out-patients building of a psychiatric hospital obviously intent on crashing through his doors.

It was after Bartholomew suggested we should make use of some form of group therapy for the use of alcohol, that we discovered it already existed and was being used widely throughout the land. And as always, we at the Institute refuse to take credit for practices which are already in existence. However, we were the first to state definitively that what many a publican witnesses every day is in fact group therapy in its natural setting and for its own logical purposes, as opposed to the perverted brain-twisting of the medical profession.

Asmolians have a predeliction for discovering other Asmolians – and where they drink. It is at these drinking places that many of us congregate for group therapy. Those who come for these beneficial treatments will be hungover, some badly. Naturally, they could obtain the necessary liquor anywhere; they choose, however, to help and be helped. Naturally, the previous evening will be discussed, but so too will be the various symptoms showing in the individual members. Condolences are exchanged and helpful advice is often given. Weak hearts who exclaim: 'I can't take it!' are encouraged to sip it slowly. Those who cannot read the paper are given the day's news by those who are sufficiently cured to do so. Late arrivals are not forced into the middle of the meeting; they are left alone to slobber in the corner. And some, so grievously wounded as to be unable to get the first drink to their lips, receive help from steadier hands. At closing time the session is considered to be over, and those who can face appointments drift off to deal with them. Those who have over-cured themselves head back to bed. All leave these therapeutic meetings feeling much better; they have spent a difficult hour or so amongst fellow sufferers and now all is well again. Common humanity will always defeat indifferent society.

Later in the day the next most common appointment pre-set for alcohol comes immediately after leaving the office. Still operating within very strict social limits, our hopeful Asmolian will stop for a drink before catching the train home, or before the tedious drive home. Three or four shots here usually keep things going until he can get home and relax over a drink. Then off for cocktails and dinner. By now the system is well stocked up and operating smoothly. General boozing can now take place without any pre-set schedule – though the night-cap is obligatory.

*

GHASTLY ACCIDENT DRINKS

Drinks taken for immediate effect.

Now that alcohol has become the most efficient fuel for the body, it is hardly surprising that when extra effort is needed to overcome disaster, this combustible, with its added tranquilizing effects, is used.

This is so obivous that there seems little point in dwelling on it overmuch. It is only a matter of degree, not of kind, between the 747 jet pilot, having dropped out of the skies and successfully churned his machine through the lounge bar, asking for a large brandy, and the housewife pouring herself a small sherry because, though disaster has not exactly struck, the phone may ring at any moment.

These sensible imbibations are now called Ghastly Accident Drinks due to Hamilton's desire recently to totally obliterate a thoroughly harrowing drive from the Institute to his mother's home in Buckinghamshire. I must point out that Hamilton's nervous system, though still in very good shape compared to most of us, was beginning to explode from time to time. On this particular occasion he came unglued through an attitude of mind which is a constant danger to us all – over-confidence. It is quite true that before leaving the Institute he stoked up at the Cocktail Lounge. In fact he was quite tight as he bumped his Maserati down the tortuous path. However, it was almost midnight as he left the outskirts of London. An hour later the drink began to die on him.

This is where over-confidence almost killed Hamilton Hamilton. Thinking he was safe, secure, snug in his fog of booze, he neglected to put the emergency half-bottle in the glove compartment. I can't emphasise too strongly how careful we must all be in this regard; sobriety could strike at any moment, and usually does so when least expected. Poor Ham slipped into the ab-dabs with every pub in the country bolted up. There was any amount of drink in his mother's house, but could he get there before the hidden horrors boomed into his mind? Already the car was getting increasingly and claustrophobially smaller, and though the traffic became progressively thinner he knew that the sanity rate was dropping. Lorries charged out at him from empty fields, oncoming traffic swerved over into his lane, pedestrians kept throwing themselves at his front bumpers and up ahead cows were stumbling out into the road. Either he stop the car and run off into the trees or he must press on to the only available drink. The Maserati sped into Buckinghamshire at one hundred and forty miles per hour.

Two hours of the heebies and Hamilton had lost control of his mind. The entire car was full of panic as he slashed up to the front door of the house. He fumbled his frame out of the car and entered the house preposterously, his limbs dangling and shaking, his eyes darting from object to object.

'Hamilton!' his gracious mother exclaimed. 'You don't look at all well.'

Hamilton was at the sideboard, rattling amongst the bottles. He pumped brandy into a glass goblet and began gulping it down.

'Hamilton!' his mild mother repeated. 'That's brandy!'

The liquor seemed to have no kick to it, no taste. It was as if he were drinking tap water. But it was brandy all right; he began to refill the goblet.

'Mother,' he announced as he returned the glass to his face. 'I've just seen a ghastly accident.'

To a very real extent, this was quite true. It was an accident and the use of the word 'ghastly' was only euphemistic.

'You weren't involved, Hamilton? Is the car all right?'

'I'm fine, mother,' Hamilton replied, gulping.

'Tell me all about it. What happened?'

Hamilton wasn't really up to this; furthermore, his mind was now racing from the very depths of the horrors to the dizzy heights of loopy-land. He poured the remainder of the bottle into the goblet:

'I'd rather not talk about it at the moment. What I need is a drink.'

'A *drink*, Hamilton. That's brandy, dear.'

'It was awful,' Hamilton was telling the wall. 'Too awful.'

'Come and sit down, dear boy. I've never seen you drink like that. I'm sure it can't be good for you. Now sit down here in the arm chair. That's it. Stretch out your feet.'

'Awful,' moaned Hamilton into the half empty goblet. 'Simply ghastly.'

'How very unpleasant for you. These things can be so upsetting. I quite understand your not wanting to talk about it. You poor boy. Let me make you some hot chocolate.'

But Hamilton poured down the rest of the brandy, let the goblet roll gently on the floor, leaned back and passed into unconsciousness.

Admittedly this may be a bit advanced for some of you. But remember that Hamilton has now progressed to a very professional standard. The point is that you should not be using alcohol for any such damned fool reason as enjoying a meal or passing a convivial hour or so with your friends. If anything upsets you, then that is a ghastly accident. Bang it in.

*

PRE-DRINK DRINKS

Alcohol taken to change the metabolism for further consumption.

Mr Emery Brown was just a trifle displeased that his wife had been asked to the Cocktail party. For one thing, in order to collect her, he had to get home immediately after work. This meant rush hour traffic, in which he now found himself. Besides, Janet did not enjoy these things. She always seemed to be nervous in the company of his employers and on occasions appeared to have been badly affected by the drink. These wretched parties were bad enough without having to keep an eye on her. On top of it all, due to the rushing, he had missed his usual drinks after work.

He wheeled the car into his drive-way and up to the garage. He went into the house through the side-door and paused in the kitchen. Janet would certainly not be ready, so he poured himself a long scotch to prepare himself for the evening ahead. He took his drink upstairs and found his wife still soaking in the bath, reading a glossy magazine, a long scotch resting on the bathtub.

'Come on, love. Up and at 'em. We'll be late.'

'I'll hurry,' replied his wife, sloshing forward in the water to get her drink. 'I know I have to appear at these things, but it is depressing. Pour us another drink, darling. To get us in the mood.'

'You're right,' Emery agreed, collecting his wife's glass. 'It is going to be pretty awful. No sense walking into it cold. All that sordid drinking.'

In the kitchen Mr Brown quickly finished his drink and began to refill the glasses. The more he thought about it the more unpleasant the evening seemed. It would be one idiotic conversation after another for at least an hour. Then, just as the drinks were beginning to work, some fool would get drunk and bore everyone home. He took the drinks up to his wife.

'Get those clothes on in a hurry, love,' he told his wife. 'Then we'll have time to stop for one on the way. I don't think I could face that boozey scene without a bracer.'

This is excellent. I have read you this little story to show you the Asmolian discipline at its easiest and most fruitful. The Browns know unconsciously what alcohol is all about. They know the futility of going to a party sober. That is not what it is all about. They also realise that their systems need priming so that they can be in the right mood to drink.

There are many examples of unconscious Asmolians doing the correct things by instinct. Many a man will arrive early for a meeting at a bar. He'll do the sensible thing and have two or three under his belt before his companions arrive. Another person, knowing that his wife has asked friends in for drinks, will break his journey home by stopping at the local for a healthy topping up. Often a number of people will have the same idea and arrange to meet in a pub before going on to a party. Whether they know it or not, they are fortunate enough to be following good Asmolian principles and with any luck will arrive at the party well stewed. In fact, if there are one or two trained Asmolians amongst them, they may not get to the party at all, bu have one of their own after the pubs have shut.

Some of you may wonder why I have not included secret drinking in this list. The simple reason is that, while it may be a hopeful sign, it is hardly a successful stage. In fact it is a sign that the malignant and unhealthy pressures of our society are extracting a terrible price from you. However, if this is the only way you are able to get sufficient alcohol into the system, then let me give you a few hints which we have found to be most efficient. Do bear in mind, though, that you simply must break out of your social prison sooner or later.

*

The Lavatory Cistern. I know it's a joke, but it does work. It is very seldom indeed that anyone goes rooting around in these things. However, so widely known is this method that once someone suspects you are drinking secretly they may inspect this hideaway first. Thus it should only be used sparingly, on a temporary basis. If you go to bed knowing you are going to to need a cure and that none will be available, then sink a flask in the cistern. Dress first, drink the flask and slip the empty into your jacket or handbag.

The Perfect Hote, Guest or Barman. Be all these things. As Host, carry drinks around for your guests. Every trip to the kitchen is a small one for yourself. The Perfect Guest, of course, is the one who moves about the room, conversing with all and mixing with everyone. This moving about will result in your being offered drinks all over the room. As you are constantly on the move, no one will notice that you are sinking about six drinks to their one. But the Barman is the best of all possible positions. Most people look upon the Barman as a 'worker' not a 'drinker'. There is no need here for elaborate techniques, such as placing the most popular beers under the temporary bar, then quaffing a secret gin as you crawl under for the beer. The simplest method is to wait until someone at the party asks for your kind of drink, then pour three or four at once, handing him only one. Frightfully easy.

The Early Arrival. This has already been mentioned but is well worth repeating. When meeting with your friends for a drink, get there first. Bang in a few doubles, then relax and drink normally with them. Occasionally this may lead to remarks about your getting so drunk so quickly, when all you had was a few beers. If these incidents occur too frequently, you may have to develop a 'diabetic tendency'. Complain to your doctor about it: sudden cravings for sugar, dizziness, palpitations, and occasionally feeling very tight on just a few beers. If he bothers to test you, don't worry; these things come and go. He'll advise you to keep an eye on your drinking! The point is that you are now quite free, after two beers, to crash out the bar room door and stumble into the traffic. It's the old sugar level acting up again.

Barman's Wink. This will hardly be necessary at your local, for there you will already have things arranged. In strange pubs make sure you buy the first round. A quiet word with the barman will ensure that whenever you wink your glass will get a double. Most barmen are extremely astute at this, often covering up the difference by using different shaped glasses or gushing the soda into yours as he hands it to you. And if you notice someone in another group at the end of the bar giving you a respectful nod, then watch carefully when his next drink is served – ten to one the tonic will be gushing into his gin. Asmolians are everywhere.

The Urgent Call. The only use the pub telephone serves is to get you out of your own company for a moment and into the next bar where you down a large one. No barman in any civilized English-speaking country will remark upon your drinking in two bars at once. When first you adopt this technique you may be self-conscious enough to actually telephone whoever it was you said you had to phone. After a while you will drop this. The line was engaged or out of order or there was no reply or the God damned Post Office should be completely reorganised. If the telephone is in *your* bar, then wait until someone is on it before remembering your urgent call. It's all very easy.

The Wine Connoisseur. Not only do you order the wine for dinner, you dispense it. Always make a great show of ensuring that everyone's glass is full: it takes less plonk to fill a half-full glass. Yours of course, is always empty. And never, never have the bottle run empty while filling your own glass. Make a good joke of squeezing the last drop into some other poor bugger's glass, then discreetly order the next bottle.

These are only six of the more common forms of secret drinking. There are many more and you will invent some of your own. I think the point to remember here is that secret drinking is a tortuous exercise forced upon you by the ignorance of your present company. Take heart, this will all change.

Aside from secret drinking, the five first signs of hope which I have outlined here all point in one direction: your metabolism is moving towards alcohol and you now need more of the stuff faster and more often than the sea of mediocrity about you. Whether you know it or not, you're on the great road to freedom and bliss. You are, in fact, an Asmolian.

Letter From an Asylum

Ladies and Gentlemen: It is true that from time to time those who have undertaken an Asmolian way of life do end up, permanently or temporarily, at society's mercy. An Asmolian, by being free and by being seen to enjoy his freedom and his personal happiness – his individual exhaltation – constitutes an antithesis to mass regulation. And to his great peril, he also constitutes a very real threat, insomuch as others may emulate him; in which case the security, and especially the emotional security, of those engaged in buttressing the fiction of organised society, is undermined. To give expression to your individual personality is to invite incarceration.

Nowadays, in such highly organised societies as our own and that of the United States and Russia, the most convenient and effective form of incarceration is in a mental institution. It is all hugely convenient; there need be no trial and therefore no embarrassing evidence. No arrest is required and thus possible dissidents within the forces of law and order are left to trouble themselves with other matters. For once a man has been locked up in a mental institution he is forever silenced and reduced to ineffectuality; he may escape, he may smuggle manuscripts out of the country and vast liberal movements may organise on his behalf. But it is all futile, for his sanity has been impugned by the highest authority in the land – the medical profession.

All this is perfectly logical. We have organised and protected our society against two forms of internal subversion. We have rules of conduct which we call laws. Those breaking these rules are punished and are either fined or sent to prison. There are others, though, who without necessarily breaking those rules, cannot accept the basic assumptions from which they were made. By the definition of the word sane, these persons must be declared insane. And as it is not the rules or laws themselves which are involved here, the question of punishment or imprisonment does not arise. And so no trial is necessary, no due process of law. As the issue involved is so profound that it must be simple, so the method of dealing with it is equally simple. The medical profession is asked to declare the man insane – which by definition he is – and he is dragged off to an asylum.

(Yes, the doctors *are* asked. Whoever heard of a psychiatrist bumping into a stranger in the streets and calling for a vehicle to have him taken away and locked up? Yet policemen are doing it every hour they are on duty.)

I don't wish to go too far into these matters, Ladies and Gentlemen. Political theory and social philosophy are best left to those impotent to effect the issues. Those of us with a job must get on with it, and with this in mind I think this would be as good a time as any to read to you Bartholomew Kent's second letter. You will remember that in his first letter he offered to give us what information and advice he could on incarceration. These then, are his words:

My dear Professor,

Thank you for your letter which, though short, conveyed to me what you wished to say. I doubt if it meant very much to them at the 'sorting office'. But for me, as each phrase revealed itself to me in its true meaning, it was a hand reaching for mine through the indestructible bars of my silent prison. Thank you.

I shall not bother to write this letter in code or double meaning. Yours coming in received but a cursory glance; mine going out will be scrutinised by eyes trained to rivet on the hidden meaning. Instead, I shall someday have it smuggled out to you. In the meantime it is my secret scroll and the only anchor I have to the sanity which they are trying to wash out of my system.

I will never know, now, how I came to be here. They, of course, have their version, and for all I know it may contain a great deal of truth. As I say, I will never know, for their drugs have erased forever the confidence one usually places in personal memory.

They tell me, though, that I arrived by taxi and that I stumbled to the front hall desk and asked for a doctor. Immediately I was a card, a file, a number and a dossier – for my arrival was noted. I'm told that in an adjoining room I explained to the doctor that I had not slept for sixteen days and seventeen nights. Then I am supposed to have woozed in and out of consciousness, sometimes rational, sometimes incoherent. I was unable, they tell me, to sign the necessary papers required to be a voluntary patient. Instead, two psychiatrists signed documents of quite a different nature.

I have no memory of this. My memory commences in a solitary room with sunlight sloping through the window. A nurse has me by the arm and is levering me to a sitting position on the bed. Then she eases me forward and I stumble into a chair in front of the simple dressing table. There is a tray of food before me; porridge, eggs, sausages, tea. The drug insulin has taken effect and my hunger is compulsive. But the sodium amytal is also in control of me and I slobber at the gruel and stuff the eggs into my mouth. I'm exhausted as I pour the tea down my throat. The nurse takes the cup from my mouth, puts a collection of pills into my hands, and together we wash the lot down. Then she helps me, strong girl, back into the sweaty bed where now a doctor stands. The rubber tape is quickly around my upper arm and he feels my elbow gently before scooping the needle into my vein. Not only is this my first memory, it is my only memory as again and again, for how many days I do not know, the ritual is repeated.

There are also other disjointed memories, mostly visual. The high lavatory walls, tiled and cracked, with the small metal panelled windows letting in only a greyish light. The pyjama cord always dragging on the ground and the constant smell of polished floors. Windows which only open eight inches and numerous doors which are locked. Then waking up again as a nurse turns me to the food on the table and the doctor waits with his needle.

Mercifully the memories of the wall opposite my bed are fading. Time is meaningless and misleading when describing the agony of staring at a blank wall, unable to move, unable to pull one's mind together, unable to comprehend or to fight. How long does terror last?

After a very long time conditions began to change. However, it would be savagely wrong to think in terms of improvement. The dosage of drugs was reduced and with this came the ability to stand and to walk. I would stroll down to the communal lounge and sit in my pyjamas and dressing gown. There were others sitting there, much the same as I. One or two were dressed and appeared to be reading. There was the odd nod – the nod of one defeated prisoner of war to another. Only one or two attempts were made at casual conversation: those in the same condition as myself could hardly understand each other. And those who had been in longer and were on fewer drugs, did not offer to talk. Perhaps they knew that it would be impossible to explain what was coming to us.

It came one day as I gazed at the tree outside my window. My mind was active enough to think and to comprehend what had happened to me. And instead of the agony of the drugs came the swelling uncontrollable anguish which no man can suffer for long. Beyond the tree and over the walls life continued as if I was still part of it. But I was no longer part of it at all: I had been removed. I was a pair of sightless eyes behind a wall. When death comes, this will be the anguish.

It was at about this time that Dr Ashbourne began to see me regularly. Of course, every day some doctor or other would have a look at me, but Dr Ashbourne's sessions, twice a week, were in private. The discussions were friendly and we talked of many things. Then one day there were two strange doctors in his office and I made the first of many, many mistakes. The second doctor asked me if I thought I was an alcoholic.

'Is that your opinion?' I asked.

'We think you are.'

'Then I accept the diagnosis.'

'Yes,' the same doctor went on. 'But are you *convinced*?'

'Gentlemen,' I told them. 'I'm not a doctor. You are. If you say there is something wrong with me then I accept your expert opinion.'

'That's not the point,' he repeated very forcibly. 'Do you admit it yourself?'

'Admit?' I queried. 'There's nothing to admit. If you tell me I have diabetes, T.B. or a common cold, I must accept what you say.'

'This isn't good enough!'

Later Dr Ashbourne was to explain to me that I had made a grave mistake. I pass on his words for those who may find themselves in a similar situation.

'Bart,' he told me, 'your answers to the senior psychiatrist didn't do you much good. You must remember that this institution is like a sausage factory, and each sausage has a dossier. Now dossiers are efficient, and for your own good always remember they exist. Now in your dossier it says that on your first interview you were unco-operative.'

'Unco-operative?'

'I know you think that's strange, Bart. But remember this is a factory. Certain things are expected of you. You're supposed to react in an anticipated fashion. And Bart, nobody just accepts alcoholism as a simple diagnosis. Not just like that. You're expected to fight it, deny it. Rationalize your way out of it. Say you're just a heavy social drinker. Scream. Shout. Lie. But not just sit there saying we're the experts and so you accept what we say.'

'But you are doctors. You are diagnoticians specialising in this field.'

'And you're an alcoholic. And you're not behaving like one.'

'A black mark in my file?'

'I'm afraid so, Bart.'

This should give you some idea of how careful one has to

be. I wouldn't be at all surprised if my rational behaviour has not set back my release by about six months.

But even worse was to happen. The full tragedy of it cannot be appreciated unless you bear in mind that ever present and all important dossier. The doctors told me I was to relax, to do anything I felt like doing. Just rest and get better, they said. Well, I must have been reading my Euclid during my sleepless nights before ending up here. The drugs were so heavy that reading was difficult. In any case, it was a warm afternoon and I went outside in the gardens to read. I wanted to lie down to read but could find no comfortable spot. Instead I found a branch in one of the trees which seemed perfectly suited to sleeping and dozing. And so I lay in the tree trying to read my Euclid.

It's hardly surprising that I went to sleep. That's what the drugs are for. Unfortunately I did not wake up for tea. I was missing. A search was made. No Bartholomew Kent. Panic button. The police were informed. The patients were excited and the doctors upset. Later in the evening one of the nurses going off duty noticed me on my branch. I was woken up and sent to bed. That may not appear tragic: what is tragic is the notation in my dossier:

THE PATIENT DID NOT MANAGE TO ESCAPE. HE WAS FOUND UP A TREE READING EUCLID.

There is a fellow here called Smythe who must have an equally black mark in his dossier. I suspect that it will be some time before he is released. He did not realise where he was when he first woke up at about four in the morning. It was a strange room and quite understandably he assumed that he had woken up in yet another strange hotel bedroom. Well, we all know what to do under those circumstances: first get a drink and then start to sort things out. As he could find no telephone for room service he wandered out of his room into what he imagined was a corridor. It was full of beds with people sound asleep. This indeed called for a drink and he was pleased to see what he thought was a uniformed member of the night staff approaching him.

'Hello there,' he said with some relief, putting his arm on her shoulder. 'I'd like you to go downstairs to the bar and get me a long gin and tonic.'

He was explaining about the ice when he found himself being led back into his room and being given some pills by the nurse. Unable to comprehend what kind of hotel he had landed in, he duly took the pills and went to sleep for about a day.

As one day is exactly the same as the next they become rather meaningless and slip by aimlessly. The important part of any day, of course, is the visit by the doctors. Incredible efforts are made to appear fit and well, but it is really of little use. Their drugs make one look goofy and disorientated – in fact, totally unsuitable for discharge.

I tried to explain all this to Dr Ashbourne. How the hell, I asked him, could one pull oneself together when the drugs were pulling one to pieces.

'We want you to relax, Bart,' he told me gently. 'Convalesce, build yourself up bodily. This sedation won't last forever. We just don't want you suffering any anxiety.'

'But what could be more frustrating than trying to read the paper and finding that you have just read the same sentence six times. And still not understand what the hell it's all about.'

'Be patient, Bart,' he explained, and for the first time I sensed that perhaps he did not fully agree with the system. 'We'll be reducing your drugs very shortly now. But while you are here, Bart, take advantage of what the place has to offer. Go to the lectures. You'll learn something about yourself.'

Well, I went to the lectures and to the group meetings. It's quite terrible what they're doing, Professor. They are deliberately undoing all the good work you've done. They're reversing your system! The lecturers try to convince us that alcohol is *bad* for us. At the group meetings, always chaired by one of the medical indoctrinaires, people are made to *confess*. Others are encouraged to make resolutions of an absurd nature. And they're so indoctrinated, what with the drugs and constant reiteration of the evils of drink, that they truly believe they are doing themselves some good by resolving never to drink again.

But the worst was to come. I was asked whether or not I would submit to Aversion Therapy. Dr Ashbourne explained it to me, and looking back now I realise he was trying to tell me not to take it.

'It's a form of treatment, Bart, designed to break down your conditioned relationship with alcohol. It was devised by a pair of doctors at the Shadel Sanitarium in America. A Dr Voegtlin and a Dr Lemere devised a series of injections which will sensitize your nervous system so that you can see for yourself just how harmful alcohol is. Now this is a voluntary treatment, Bart. You're in no way obliged to undergo it.'

'But I'll get out faster if I do.'

This seemed to put Ashbourne in a difficult situation. He fumbled for a moment, then replied hesitatingly,

'Co-operation is always noted, Bart. But you can't really be expected to co-operate to the point of submitting yourself to treatment in the wrong frame of mind. Normally, it shouldn't make one damn bit of difference whether you take this treatment or not. But Bart, I have to be honest with you here. Your record does show a certain lack of co-operation. I know the meetings are open to discussions. But constructive discussion, Bart. Not tirades from you on the wickedness of the medical profession. And I suppose Bart, although it should not be this way, I suppose your volunteering for aversion therapy would at least show to those who decide on your discharge, that you were trying to get better.'

'But surely you decide on my release.'

'Not entirely, Bart. Not entirely. We confer amongst ourselves.'

'A committee! A damned Committee decides whether people are to be locked up or set free.'

'It's the best way, Bart. The only way, really. We don't want relapses.'

Mark well those words, Professor, and pass them on to all who may suffer incarceration at the hands of doctors. For it is not a question of one dossier: there are two. The second dossier relates to the doctors themselves. Each has a career to protect and each has a record with which he hopes to further that career. Someday, when being considered for advancement, their dossiers will be compared. Those whose patients tend to 'relapse' do not receive consideration; those with only a few 'relapses' against them are given some thought; those without a single 'relapse' find themselves elevated to positions of administrative authority. This organisational system must be borne in mind by all those who wish to remain sane in an asylum. You are there because your emotional make-up disturbs the tranquil dreams of a complacent society. You are not there to get well: you are there to conform to the tranquil dream. And 'successful treatment' does not relate to your well-being: it has nothing at all to do with you. It is a notation in a doctor's, or group of doctors', record. And you will stay in an asylum until such time as those responsible for your discharge are confident that you will never in the future constitute a threat to their advancement. That, Professor, is what psychiatry is all about.

Dr Ashbourne himself must have been beginning to realise all this, for he never appears at my aversion therapy treatments. These are conducted on the floor above me. I am asked to change into my pyjamas and then given my injection. In the asceptic little room upstairs I am met by a Dr Moorhead, a man I meet on no other occasion. There is a table with two chairs. There is also a sink. On the table there are four or five plastic glasses of various liquors.

'Good evening, Mr Kent,' he says each time. 'Do sit down and relax. At the risk of boring you, I'm going to repeat what this treatment is all about and how it is going to help you.

'To begin with, there is a conditioned association in your mind between alcohol and a feeling of well-being. Now this is neither unusual or startling. Over the years your body has learnt, in the very real sense of physical learning, that alcohol is a pleasant drug which will do you the world of good. This lesson has been learnt well and has been confirmed so often that reason alone cannot help you to understand that it is totally fallacious.

'Exactly the same thing happens with cigarette smokers. When feeling groggy in the morning the first thing they do is attempt to make themselves feel better by introducing an appallingly toxic and dangerous drug – a drug which at one time was nauseous. But the smoker does not feel nauseated because his mind has been telling him for years that it is a pleasant sensation. You can understand then, Mr Kent, that if we could return smokers to the condition under which they had their first cigarette then they would stop smoking immediately. We can't do that yet. We just don't have the drugs for purifying the nervous system to its pre-addictive state in the case of nicotine.

'But we can do it with alcohol. The injection which you have just received has sensitized your nervous system to a condition which obtained when you were a young teenager. As you sit here now, Mr Kent, you might just as well have never had a drink in your life. All the in-built protective conditioning has gone. Have a drink now and you will experience alcohol as it really is, not as your mind has masked it. You'll find your favourite drink there. That's Scotch on the right. But I'd like you to taste them all. For it would be wrong for you to learn that Scotch alone is a vile chemical. The whole lot, Mr Kent, every form of alcohol is poison.'

With this I look at the drinks. They're in rather unattractive translucent containers. One or two are obviously beer. The rest are undiluted spirits. I reach for the Scotch and take a healthy sip. It's bloody marvellous!

'You're probably enjoying that,' the good doctor is explaining. 'This is to be expected. You've developed a taste for it and there is nothing we can do about your taste buds. But what about your stomach, Mr Kent? How is your stomach reacting to this chemical?'

'Feels rather warm and nice, actually. In fact it feels as if a long lost friend has come home again.'

'That is the conditioning to which I referred. But it won't last. Soon your stomach and your head will begin to tell you just what it really is you've given them. For though your mind may tell you it's a good idea, Mr Kent, your stomach does not like to be poisoned. Nor do the arteries in your head care for the assault upon your brain. Try some of the other drinks. Taste them properly – for what they really are.'

This I do. The beer is rather fun, if warm. One of them is a stout, which I don't really care for. Very gingerly I sip at the rum, a drink I've always considered distasteful. Then back to the Scotch, my friend, my other half.

'You're not finding that stuff quite so pleasant, are you Mr Kent? You don't really like any of them except the Scotch. In fact they're all equally awful, but you've trained yourself to think otherwise of the Scotch. Yet even that, Mr Kent, is beginning to taste unpleasant. Am I correct?'

'You may have something there. I still like the Scotch, but I'm not feeling all that well. But then I never do at these sessions.'

'These sessions, Mr Kent, are *reality*. You are now taking alcohol in your normal pristine state, uncluttered by conditioning and unreal associations.'

'Well, I'd just as soon stop drinking now, if it's all the same to you. I know what's coming.'

'You know *now*, Mr Kent. But in two days, two weeks, two months, and your memory of unpleasantness will go. We have to forget unpleasant things, Mr Kent, or we'd all go mad. But when *you* forget, you substitute a memory of pleasure. Now I'm here to help you. To help you unlearn that fiction and re-learn the reality of drink. As a doctor and as a disinterested Samaritan, I urge you to continue drinking. *Learn*, Mr Kent. Teach yourself again what booze really is.'

And so I drink some more Scotch. But I'm dreading it, Professor. I know what's coming. Shall I try to describe it to you now, now that (as the doctor maintains) all memories of pain and unpleasantness are passed and euphoric substitutions (as the doctor explained) are in operation.

To be as clinical and as objective as possible:

At first, and for some time, a distinct feeling of ill health. Things are not as they should be; suddenly you've smoked a hundred and forty two cigarettes, eaten six hot dogs and drunk four bottles of tainted lime juice. Your eyes are strained from reading 'War and Peace' in paperback and your neck has been left in the deep freeze overnight. Somebody has severed the tendons behind your knees and you need a friend. The pains in your head go through a controlled explosion before dribbling down your throat into your stomach. And that's where the trouble starts.

At first you're just sick by burping: belch, and its on your pyjamas. Your friendly doctor leaves for a moment and returns with a nurse who most kindly wipes up the worst from your chest. But the room has gone all to hell, skew-wiff and tilted, as you lurch to the sink. You don't make it and lie on the floor burping and belching vomit into your face and on to your pyjamas and into the crisp uniform of the nurse who is turning you over on to your stomach so that you don't choke in your own puke.

'Now, Kent, this is what alcohol is all about. You're healthy and clean, and this is what it does to a healthy, clean person. Are you able to learn, Kent? LEARN, LEARN, LEARN. It's the dirtiest poison you've ever poured into your system. By the way, you've just evacuated your bowels into your pyjama bottoms!'

You try to lie there because he is trying to help. But the cramps in your gut have started. You're not even puking: you're just making noises, sitting upright on the floor.

'Ah, ah, ah.'

But you can't move. Like any other sick person you hold on to the nurse's arm and hold on tight. Your hand is removed. Back to the wall.

'Of course you want help, Kent. But what help can be given to a man who has just deliberately taken poison. Deliberately taken it, Kent. And not for the first time. For the thousandth time. But now you're getting it as it really is. Kent, listen to me. Every time you're out on the piss you're doing this to yourself. But it's all covered up. You still pay the penalty, only it's a day later, or two days later. Or years later. But now, Kent, *NOW*, you're getting it for real. Learn Kent. Listen. I'm here to help you to be sick and to learn. You're sick, Kent. You're sick all over the place.'

What you learn is that snot comes out of your nose and hangs there. You learn that you cannot control your ass and it's all over the place. You learn that the nurse is there for an arm to hold on to: not for a handkerchief or a mop-up. You learn that from beginning to end your existence is a tube running from your mouth to your anus and that is you from beginning to end.

And when you can move no more, when the muscles won't chuck any more, then you're given the pills. Unable really to stand, you're led down the stairs to your room. You're eased back into bed, still burping a tasteless, bubbly fluid. The pills hit you like sleeping gas; you're rolled on to your stomach and you moan into oblivion.

Well, Professor, that is their system. In terms of human achievement I do not know what this sort of treatment or any such treatment might attain. I dare say that a great deal of their logic is sound. If you want to get rats to copulate on the sound of the Angelus it can be done. Mechanistically all is possible.

But there is one flaw, Professor. And this flaw lies not with the system, but with the man – because they *are* men. Or, at least one or two are. I refer in particular, needless to say, to Dr Ashbourne, who was never present at these treatments.

'Well, Bart,' he said to me on what was immediately to become the most significant day of my life. 'How are you getting on with the Aversion Therapy?'

'Stupid question,' I replied. 'You know. You know from your text books what should happen. And you know from the report in your drawer what did happen. But I don't have the text books and I don't have your report. So you tell me. What do I say to get out of here?'

Professor, for a full minute the poor bugger just sat there, playing with the same piece of paper. He folded it. He unfolded it. He looked at it. Then he put it to one side. Then he picked up his appointment book. He looked at this blankly. He put it down. He looked at me and then at his desk. Then he told me:

'Bart, for Christ's sake, just between you and me? No further, Bart.'

'Agreed.'

'It wouldn't have mattered, Bart. It wouldn't have mattered if you drank Coca Cola or cyanide. You were injected with Apamorphine. You would have puked your guts up on milk.'

We both sat there stunned for a moment. I with the new information, he with his treason.

'Bart,' he said with the voice of defeat. 'Obviously we're both in trouble. Let's help each other to get the hell out of this place.'

For some reason this did not come to me as any great shock. It may well be that when the human mind is surrounded by organised madness it is well aware of the fact without being in the least inclined to face it. Many people ask, and one still hears the question: how could the Jews have gone into the chambers without a fight? This is probably the answer, or a goodly part of it. It is impossible to accept that an entire Institution or system is utterly mad while at the time it is exhibiting every indication of orderly and methodical organisation. Somehow the chamber *is* a device for fumigating lice. Somehow doctors who have spent their entire adult life studying the human personality must have retained their humanity. But when faced with the fact that this is not necessarily so, it comes as no great shock.

'Dr Ashbourne,' I said rather formally. 'Resign.'

'On what grounds? Medical? Then I cease to practise medicine. Ethical? Moral? A matter of conscience? Bart, they'd think I was mad.'

'Then fight from *within* the system. Get the odd poor bugger out. Falsify an entry in someone's dossier. Keep yourself sane by fighting for those who are.'

'We work in conference, Bart. By consultation. We're a team.'

'Then get ME out.'

In his own defeated sort of way he played again with the paper on his desk. He seemed to be thinking of other things as he spoke:

'I can get you out, Bart. For a start, I'd like you to begin with some sort of vague religious feelings. Nothing too definite. Just an understanding that there is a power greater than yourself. Then I want you to continue with the Aversion Therapy. After this, realise that you are powerless where drink is concerned and that no amount of will power is going to make any difference. Then discover that this power greater than yourself can save you from drinking. After this you will attend a few A.A. meetings, get the message but still remain humble in the face of what alcohol could do to you. Explain all this to anyone who will listen, but always make the point that you want to return regularly to this Asylum for guidance. Do these things, Bart, and we'll have you out in no time.'

'And you?'

'Personally, I'm going to write myself a prescription. Nothing too drastic. Just a little something to ease the sharp corners of reality.'

Well, Professor, I had found a friend. And this is very important for those who find themselves in places such as this. Search out the doctor who is not quite as cocky or regimented as the others. In the course of conversation, bring him gently round to discussing his problem with the Asylum. There is a very good chance that he may be sane and, feeling pretty dreadful about the incongruity of it all, may agree to help. Herein lies your only hope.

Most of the days, as I've said, pass with staggering monotony. Cases arrive for massive sedation and are put in the rooms at the end of the ward. After a few days we see them stumbling about looking for water or the lavatory or, in a few notable cases, the exit.

Escape, of course, is impossible. Even if one were to devise a foolproof scheme for getting through all the check points and all the locked doors (some are trying but they're in a haze of Largactil) where do you go? The police immediately have your description and a list of places you are likely to visit for help. And without money and with only half a mind, how do you elude the police, fight the State and feed yourself for the necessary time it takes public opinion to force them to reconsider the possibility of your sanity.

My final black mark came about a week ago. You will understand, Professor, that there are occasions when they get these drugs all wrong. We are all different; and standard dosage is indicated for an average man – that statistical fiction. Sometimes an overdose puts some poor bugger into a semi-coma, other times a depressive is lifted into farcical mania. And quite often the process of withdrawal is carried out too quickly and then strange things can happen.

I was looking out of my window at the time. To say that I suffered an attack of despair is simply to write down useless words. It is far easier and more accurate to describe it in terms of the tree outside my window. I found myself very rapidly becoming aware that the tree was sane and that it would remain so for ever. The bloody doctors, if they could, would certify it immediately; but they had overlooked it and would continue to do so as long as they had their own fellow creatures to work on. And the tree would be there long after I had gone, after others had come and gone, after we'd all gone and the doctors had been buried. It was a simple form of life which we had not yet contaminated with self-analysis, degrees in mental diagnosis, hypnotic drugs or the authority to incarcerate. I was sobbing on my bed when they found me.

Naturally, the remedy for a patient who has for a moment looked upon reality is to knock him to hell out of reality. And so I was duly drugged up to the back teeth and sent wobbling on my way. And a notation was made in some dossier to the effect that some patient was not yet emotionally strong enough to stand up to the diagnosis that he is an alcoholic.

Professor, I think I will end this letter now. There seems to be little more to add that might be of use to you or to your patients. Something has happened today which I find very disturbing and all I can say is that I think I have lost hope.

One of the 'arrival' rooms at the end of the ward has been empty for a day or two. Naturally enough, we try to find out what kind of patient will next be admitted. Sometimes we sneak in to see what his clothes are like. We ask the nurses jokingly. We watch the doctors. What the hell else is there to do here!

I myself went into the room this morning. I tried to snoop into the drawers and have a peek into the cupboard. But I soon realised that I was not alone. I turned, and there was Dr Ashbourne.

'Sorry, Doc,' I smiled. 'We always try to find out who's coming in for sedation. I'll try to get out without being seen. There's no need for a report, is there?'

But the doctor did not reply. I left the room quietly and returned to my lounge. At lunch it was learned that the patient had been sedated. And I sat there like a fool unable to let the penny drop. All afternoon I've been edgy and not known why. And sometimes I have even looked at the closed door of the room wandering why it upsets me. It wasn't until tea that my mind allowed the penny to drop into my empty stomach.

While I was in the room, while I was talking to him, Dr Ashbourne had been in the bed.

*

And now, Ladies and Gentlemen, I would like to read to you from the main front page story of the Dublin Evening Press, dated January 5, 1971:

> MENTAL HOME ESCAPE PROBE
> A full-scale investigation is being launched into the high-security Central Mental Hospital, Dundrum, where some extraordinary events took place recently, including the escape of five men, two of them last night.
>
> On Christmas Eve three men escaped using a make-shift rope which was afterwards left hanging from the wall for five days. Yesterday two others escaped by exactly the same route after beating up a warder. Only one of the escapees remains to be captured.
>
> The investigation will probe the security aspect of the institution. The grim walls of the institution are shrouded in mystery and secrecy and little information is available about what happens inside.

It has been confirmed that a young male prisoner, a convicted murderer, committed suicide in the grounds two months ago.

Typical, too, is the case of the young Maoist, Martin Dolphin, who has now been in the Hospital as a 'custody patient' for three months.

Dolphin was serving a week's sentence in Mountjoy for contempt of court when he was taken to Dundrum having been 'certified' by two doctors associated with the jail.

It is alleged that the grounds for certification have not been revealed, and that this case is an infringement of civil liberty and a misuse of professional powers made easier by strange circumstances of Dundrum.

The recent escapes once again focussed attention on the institution but here again any details of the escapees, their institutional history and what their mental state was liable to be was not available to people living in the neighbourhood, or for that matter any other members of the public.

The Department of Health today said that the escapes were under investigation and added that a special investigation by an officer of the Department was carried out into the recent suicide of a patient. This was also the subject of a Coroner's inquest.

*

I am well aware of the allegations that the sentence: 'Only one of the escapees remains to be captured' refers to Bartholomew Kent. I am equally aware of the rumours that he slipped back into England and is now being harboured, in salubrious retirement, in and by The Asmolian Institute.

It must be appreciated that I am not able to comment, nor am I at liberty to disclose how we came to have his letters.

All I can do is quote the old adage: 'We live in hope.' Unfortunately Bart himself would be – or is – the first to finish that quotation:

We live in hope, and die in despair.

Five Clinchers of Success

Ladies and Gentlemen: Just for the moment I would like to leave to one side this tiresome question of Eamonn Kelly and instead try to give you some description of what the tabloid press have come to call the 'Hell Hole of Humanity'. They are referring (if indeed they bother, journalistically, to 'refer' to anything) to Ward D.

You may remember that I mentioned in an earlier lecture the necessity from time to time of restraining the activities of some patients, both in their own interest and in the interests of staff and visitors. This is perfectly acceptable practice the world over; yet so hysterical are some of the reactions to the Asmolian Institute that several fools have shouted words like Habeas Corpus in my face. Might I remind all such reactionaries to scientific progress of the existence of Looey and Bluey, and the oblivion of Ward D.

It is quite true, of course, that what in the end turned out to be Ward D, started in the first place to be something quite different. But those working in the field of research would be blind indeed if they were unable to recognise in a constructional disaster what was in fact an architectural windfall.

I am unable now to remember whose idea it was to build a swimming pool. It may have been mine and it may have been a very good idea; the result, however, due to the viciousness of the County Council in refusing to lay on the necessary water supply, was a dry swimming pool. This being the case, it was decided to cover over the top of the pool with stiff boarding to prevent accidents.

When the question of an isolation Ward arose I'm glad to say that it was I who realised where the solution lay.

'What we need,' I told my staff, 'is a large area about the size of a dormitory. Naturally it must be isolated both physically and acoustically. It should have one entrance and no exit. Egress should be gained along gently sloping steps, preferably downward.'

Everyone agreed to this.

'Then cut a trap door over the steps at the shallow end of the empty swimming pool. This will cost about a fiver's worth of labour. Then send the entire cost of "Ward D" to the Ministry of Health.'

Now I hope it won't be necessary for me to interrupt my lectures any further with explanations of Ward D. The question I would like to press on with today is one which is always cropping up amongst my patients and may be of interest to those of you here today. I am often asked:

'But, Professor, how will I ever know that I have become a successful Asmolian?'

Now as Asmolian treatment is to such a very great extent in the hands of the patient himself, it is incumbent upon me to supply this information. However, it is no onerous duty, I assure you. It is a pleasure indeed for an instructor to inform his students of success.

Before giving you these five signs of success, though, let me take you back to our original concept of purest Asmolianism – the Alcolergic. Aside from the purity of his biochemical heredity, which can never be ours, there were two other major factors which can be ours and which we should always bear in mind. These are that, for all of us, this is a progressive path to paradise. Once we're on it we're on it for life. And the second factor to remember is that once the first stage has been reached, the actual rate of progression from one stage to another will increase. We move ever faster towards Nirvana.

Bear these in mind as we talk of the Clinchers of Success and I'm sure hope will spring from your heart.

PERSONALITY CHANGE

The appearance, in drink, of personality traits not met under other circumstances.

This may be to some degree a misnomer. It is not so much that the personality changes; rather it reverts to type. So strong and perverted are the inhibitions of society that no amount of drink will break down the persona of what is known as a normal member of the community. Intoxication will take place, definitely. Some pretty fanciful and fun-loving activity may take place – but it will all be in character. And by 'character' I refer to twenty or thirty years of high-pressured indoctrination.

On the other hand, once the metabolic system of the Asmolian has been altered by, and to, alcohol, this is no longer the case. For allied to the metabolic systems are the psychic systems, and these take their lead from metabolism once this in itself has been affected by alcohol. The results are phenomenal!

It was in this field, more than in any other, that Hamilton Hamilton was to contribute so much. You will remember Hamy's urbane personality, his flaccid manner and his generous nature. We felt these personal traits fitted him excellently for the position of Night Club proprietor; not only this, but from such a vantage point he could surely supply us with endless detailed information which might otherwise prove hard to come by. With all this in mind, and using his own money (to keep his mind involved in the job, of course) Hamilton was persuaded to open 'Hamilton's Hideaway', a very secluded night-spot indeed, situated on the top of a hill.

In one sense, I suppose, Hamilton might be likened to one or two of our original animal subjects. His behaviour and his personality balance were perfect. Now I wouldn't go so far as to say we broke Hamy down: I would go so far as to say that within six months of opening his Night Club, due to a combination of vast intakes of alcohol plus numerous visits from myself and associates, Hamy was totally freed from the iron mask of his own persona and, when drunk, reverted to type. Just what type Hamilton truly is I will try to show you by two visits I made to his establishment on the same evening.

The first visit was made with some help from Looey and Bluey who, naturally enough, were acting as 'waiters' in 'Hamilton's Hideaway'. I had asked them to supply me, for the early part of the evening, with two toughs, preferably ones with marked and volatile dislikes for the upper classes and especially any member of such class or classes who might have decided to indulge in the luxury of owning a Night Club. These arrangements were made discreetly, and quite early in the evening, when Hamilton was what might be called sober, I arrived for dinner with my two guests.

One was wearing a German officer's field coat from the First World War; the other seemed to be dressed in nothing but sheepskin – and not completely dressed, at that.

'Good evening, Hamilton,' I said as soon as he approached us. 'I didn't bother to book. Just bumped into these very good friends of mine and wondered if you could feed us. We'll go, of course, if it's inconvenient.'

'Not at all, Professor,' Hamilton beamed at me and turned to what must have been for him two of the most uncouth and positively dangerous men ever to be standing in his premises. 'And good evening to you, gentlemen. I'm always pleased when the Professor brings his friends along.'

This attempt at pleasantry was met by a silence which can only be described as rock hard. But Hamilton, nerveless, as ever, continued with his patter.

'If you gentlemen would like to give me your coats I'll show you to a comfortable table.'

The German Field Officer immediately wrapped his coat more tightly around his thin frame. But far worse, the Urban Shepherd began to loosen his, exposing yet another pelt which, were it taken out and dry cleaned, might conceivably have been human hair.

'On second thoughts,' Hamilton nodded generously, 'it might be best to leave your coats on for a moment or two. We've just opened for the evening and I feel the central heating isn't all it should be.'

'Fuck the central heating.'

'I want a shit.'

'I think you'll find this table much to your liking, Professor. It's quite secluded and you and your friends should be able to chat amiably here without being disturbed.'

'I said shit, not chat.'

'Splendid,' Hamilton agreed pleasantly. 'I'll get a waiter along to look after your every need.'

With this Hamilton graciously nodded to the three of us and moved suavely off in the direction of the bar.

The meal was a disaster. The hirsute herdsman drank his wine from the bottle; the neo-nazi finished each drink by crunching the empty glass into the ashtray. Both rejected their steaks; one on the gastronomical grounds that it was horseshit, the other on the epicurian grounds that it was uncooked horseshit.

Throughout all this Hamilton behaved with chivalry and charm. When asked how such a ponce as he ever came to own such a clipjoint as this, he replied, totally without insult, that he did not find it necessary to do a great deal of poncing and that the place could do with improvements. In fact, he said, it would help him if more of his customers were as constructive as my friends. When it came time to pay the bill, which Hamilton would not hear of, the three men were on friendly terms, vying with each other to remember the dirtiest doss-house experiences.

'Hamilton,' I said as he showed us to the door, 'I might be dropping back later in the evening. You may remember my niece Cynthia. She's in town for the weekend with her fiance. If you could keep a table . . .'

'Certainly, Professor. I'll look forward to that.'

With this I left, accompanied by my two ruffians and sent them on their way home to Trafalgar Square, or wherever it is our intellectual young sleep these days.

My niece Cynthia is a rather tall girl. She has light coloured hair, tilts her head slightly when she talks about horses and house parties, and feels very sorry for those who suffer. Charles, her affianced, is equally tall but never tilts his feline head, not even when talking about mother, and feels damnably sorry for those who were sent down from University. They are a charming couple who could give offense to no one.

I left it quite late before taking them along to 'Hamilton's Hideaway'. When we arrived, Hamilton himself was looking tired and had, in some miraculous way, become unshaven. His eyes were those of a man who has just spent three days in unsuccessful negotiations for the Palestinian refugees and the left side of his upper lip was somehow being inexorably drawn upwards towards his ear. As I introduced him to my niece it became suddenly apparent that they, as representatives of international militant Zionism, were personally and hellishly responsible for the homeless starving wraiths in refugee camps throughout the Middle East.

'My uncle has been telling us so much about you,' Cynthia was beaming. 'I'm very proud of him, you know. I feel rather honoured to meet one of his principal colleagues.'

'The Professor needs friends he can trust,' Hamilton replied in a voice that conveyed six different meanings, five of which carried the implication that I was at that moment in the wrong company.

'I believe,' Charles announced with pride, 'that his work is the most important being done in the country today.'

'And I believe,' Hamilton snarled, his left lip now twitching, 'that he has enemies. And that these enemies are closer to him than he thinks.'

'Oh, surely not,' Cynthia complained. 'I know there is some resistance, inevitable resistance, to new thinking, but surely . . .'

'You prissy snot!' Hamilton shouted. 'At best you're an ignorant cunt on a horse four times more intelligent than yourself. But there's more to you and your simpering lackey there. I have half a mind to slap your teeth in.'

'Hold on, here,' Charles murmured. 'There's been some misunderstanding.'

'Yes, there has,' Hamilton echoed ominously. 'And I'm about to have it sorted out.'

With this he marched off in the direction of Looey and

Bluey. But long before they could arrive, my charming dinner companions had fled to their hotel.

THE BLACK OUT

A breakdown in memory, during which time other systems continue to function.

To pass out at a party is a very good thing. To be so blind drunk that you cannot know what is going on is excellent. To crash, unconscious, into your host's Dresden collection shows that you are doing the right thing. To be carted home, insensible, is evidence of effort. And to have no memory of these events is natural and merciful: but it is not, in itself, a clincher of success.

It is better by far that you wake up, not totally without memory, *but with gaps.* To remember the drive home, the route you took and the difficulty of getting the car into the garage, but unable to remember where you came *from* – this is success. To have negotiated for your firm a profitable contract, but not remember the meeting – this is glory. These are instances of 'black-outs' and indicate that, while you may have a long way to go before reaching Nirvana, your memory box is at least breaking down and releasing you from the prison of stereotype brain functions.

When one has become quite adept at black-outs, the student will begin to realise that they are happening all the time without his being aware of it. Though our brains may be wonderous and complicated pieces of machinery, there is no mechanism inside it for telling us that we have forgotten something. At this moment you do not know what was happening to you at four o'clock in the afternoon of 4th May last, and there is no part of your mind making you aware of this memory loss. Thus Asmolians wander happily about the land, remembering little and unaware that they have forgotten a great deal more.

Initially some of you may find it embarrassing to be approached by a total stranger and be greeted by name. Now this is going to happen to you all the time and there is only one way to deal with it. At first you may experiment with such stratagems as vagueness and conjecture. You will fail, I assure you. People are very sensitive about being remembered, as any student of Dale Carnegie should know, and will soon detect your hesitancy. He will then bear in mercilessly on your weak area and eventually have you reduced to the point where you have to admit that not only do you not remember him, but also that for the last fifteen minutes you have been inflicting upon him a most insulting personal fraud.

The only way out of this difficult situation is to use the technique which we have developed at the Institute. Ideally, it should be called 'The Carnegie-Potter Reverse Thrust Lever Action', but this is too much altogether and instead we use the simple term 'feed-back'. It is based first on the Carnegie principal that the person speaking to you is more interested in himself than he is in you. Secondly, Stephen Potter's contribution is the concept of 'ploy' in weak situations. Finally, by reversing the action and thrusting the blank area on to your companion, you lever from him the necessary information. Here is an ideal example:

Your name happens to be Joe and you are leaning against the bar trying to enjoy a solitary and healthy drink. An utter stranger, wearing a mackintosh, notices you, smiles, and walks straight up to you.

'Hello, Joe,' he says. 'Let me get you a drink.'

'Ah, no,' you reply. 'I think under the circumstances it is I who should be buying you a drink.'

'Well, I don't know about that. But a pint of bitter, anyway.'

It is while you are ordering this that he comes out with the deadly opener:

'Well, Joe. How did things work out in the end?'

This must be stopped immediately! Change at once into reverse thrust.

'And well you may ask,' you reply with a knowing smile. 'What is far more important is how you got on.'

'I don't quite follow.'

'You can't have forgotten *everything* about our last meeting?'

'No, of course not,' he replies, but he is weakening. 'But

I've often wondered how you got yourself out of that mess.'

'With your help, of course.'

'My help?'

'That shouldn't surprise you,' you tell him with friendship. 'You were a great help, and you know it.'

'Hell. All I did was stand around and listen.'

'You did a great deal more,' you inform him. 'I want to thank you.'

'Well, that's very nice of you, Joe. It didn't seem at the time that I could be of much use.'

'That's just like you. You help someone, you listen, you do the best thing that could be done under the circumstances, then you don't even feel you should be thanked.'

'Quite frankly, Joe, I didn't know what to advise. A mess like that . . .'

'That mess,' you state quite firmly, 'is all over. And I simply wanted to buy you a drink and thank you. Let's leave it at that, shall we?'

'Of course, Joe. Of course. Well, here's to you. I'm glad everything worked out and I'm glad to have been of some help. Here's an end to it.'

That is the feed-back system working at its best. You don't know now, and you never will know, what this fool is on about. But he will leave you thinking that you are an excellent fellow indeed, a chap who got into a spot of bother and came through it like a man. And furthermore, a man who no longer wishes to discuss the matter, That, Sir, is character.

Those of you who know the work of the American Sociologist Mr Shelley Berman, will be aware of his study in telephonic memory recall. This is a technique whereby the Asmolian attempts to fill in his black-out by use of the telephone. The case history cited by Mr Berman is that of Sam Spiro, a man with some morning problems, one of which is a black-out on the previous evening. Here is the case as Mr Berman gives it to us; I think it is a classic and for the moment gives us all the information we need on the phenomena of black-outs.

Mr Spiro has just awoken and is addressing his first remarks to his empty bedroom.

. . . Oh God, God . . . Oh God, God, God . . . Oh God, God.

My tongue is asleep . . . and my teeth itch. Where . . . where is my Alka-Selt-zer. Oh my God don't fizz! Don't be *mean*, Alka-Seltzer. Dissolve. Oh, the hell with it, I'll drink the pieces. Hail Moscow . . . Aw God, aw c'mon God, will ya.

Uses telephone

Hello there. Ah, oh Dave. Dave boy. How're you doin' there, Dave. Dave . . . I wonder . . . do you think you could whisper. It's me. It's me. It's your old buddy. It's . . . it's . . . it's . . . ah . . . ah . . . Just a minute Dave. Don't press me. If you nag at me I'll never get it. Isn't that *ridiculous*. I just got a letter this morning. Do I sound familiar at all? Do you want to take a stab at a name? I don't know . . . what letter it begins with. It's silly . . .I know my own name . . . I know it as well as I know . . . oh God. I know the name really. It's . . . ah . . . Sam! How many Sams do you know? Oh God. It's . . . ah . . . it's Sammy Spiro! Dave, that's who it is. Old Sammy Spiro. Well, let's not quibble about pronunciation. What is it – Spiro? All right. Spiro. We'll settle for that. How're you doing there fellow, how're you doing there, kid? That's good. I'm glad to hear that. Oh . . . no, not so hot, Dave. I'm a little under the weather from last night's party. I have this . . . I have this little headache in my left eye. Hm . . . ah . . . that's what I called you about . . . to thank you for that wonderful party you had last night. 'Course we brought our own liquor, but you provided the electricity. Tell me, Dave, did I have a good time? No, I don't know, Dave. From a certain point in the evening everything's a complete blank. Ha, ha. A few minutes after I arrived. What did I do? What? Oh no . . . oh God . . . ooooo boy! Oh gee, I'm sorry, Dave.

Er . . . the whole window, eh? It just came right out, eh? Yeah, that's a picture window too, ain't it, Dave? It's a lucky thing there was nobody walking under it at the time, eh? Oh? Oh . . . oh . . . ooo boy! Got 'em edgewise, huh? Oh, they'll . . . they'll put him back together again, Dave . . . those medical people are . . .

Gee, Dave, I can't imagine how I managed to break the window . . . I've no cuts or bruises on my hands. How, how did I break the window? I see . . . yeah . . . Were you very fond of that cat? You know, those things are s'posed to land on their feet, aren't they, Dave? Poor little fellow!

How did I manage to do that? Oh yeah. Yeah, I get the picture. Yeah, I must have been playing some sort of stupid game there. What was I doing? I see . . . and I guess the window was Goliath. Well, gee, Dave, naturally I'll do my best to repair your window. Well, it's a picture window, right? Well, it'll take a lot of wood and well . . . ah . . . you'll probably want a new cat, eh fella? Yeah, well, he's a gonner.

Dave I . . . ah . . . I wish you wouldn't be quite so descriptive about the cat, Dave . . . I'm not a well man, Dave . . . yeah, well first chance we get we'll bury it all. And I'm sorry. Dave, I wonder if you'd mind if we changed the subject to something a little more pleasant . . . if you don't mind . . .

Tell me – did your wife enjoy the party? What do you mean – I ought to know? I did not . . . I did not! Dave, it was a long hard party, Dave. She may have just gotten tired and stretched out for a bit . . . Well, I thought it was a pile of clothing, Dave. Dave – you know how I feel about Myrna. Why, I love your wife. Now that isn't what I meant, Dave. I mean I love your wife the same way I love you. No, that's not what I meant either. I hardly think it's necessary for you to warn me to keep my hands off you too.

What? . . . No kidding. Right off the hinges, huh? Eh . . . eh . . . the whole damn door. D'you think you can get along without it, Dave? No, that's right, your bathroom is right off your kitchen.

Dave . . . Dave . . . when you come down to it the only real damage I caused was a broken window and a broken door, right? No, I won't forget the cat, Dave.

Eh, eh . . . well, Dave, considering the shape I was in it's lucky the only thing I threw through the window was a cat, eh? Ah . . . ah . . . ah . . . Oh really! Who? Oh God . . . um . . . Hope she wasn't angry. Well, that's swell. She always was a pretty good sport, your mother. Listen, er, Dave. Dave, the reason I'm calling . . . the reason I'm . . . I'm having these business associates in town for the weekend and I'd like to throw this little shindig. You know how small my place is and I was wondering if I could use your place for a few hours Saturday night. You know what I mean, a few drinks, a coupla laughs, you know. Dave . . . ah, Dave . . . c'mon boy, pull yourself together over there. Dave, stop that! I can't bear to hear a man cry. Dave, don't call me that name. It's a reflection on my parents. Now, Dave . . . Dave . . . Dave . . .

THE INVOLUNTARY BREAKOUT

Getting drunk at the wrong time.

One of the most hopeful clinchers of success is exhibited when the body, concurring to the discovery by the personality and the confirmation in mental adjustment, breaks out on its own individual escapes of alcoholic release. This is indeed a cause for joy because one no longer has to give any thought or effort to one's studies. The Asmolian Syndrome is well in operation and can be left to take charge of behaviour in general.

Not surprisingly, a lot of our students have remarked that the first indication of this clincher appeared *at the wrong times*. It is the use of this phrase which shows so clearly just how stupid and how wicked our social taboos really are. For in terms of Asmolianism, that is to say in terms of personal happiness and release, one is in fact getting drunk *at the right time.* For some extraordinary reason, middle management throughout industry is of the impression that Board Meetings are terribly important affairs and that under no circumstances should one attend such a meeting with a trace of alcohol in one's system. Yet there are countless examples of executives in the middle range of management bracing themselves with one or two stiff ones before going to these débâcles. And those with healthy Asmolian Syndromes will find that the one or two drinks which they were going to have at lunch extend themselves, quite involuntarily, into an afternoon session, with the result that the fortunate executive arrives at the Board Meeting out of his mind with drink, unable to remember his facts or even why he is there. I say fortunate, for if the firm is any damned good its Directors will immediately recognise a man of their own calibre, as they too will be enjoying the release the Asmolian body gives to these occasions and will be stewed beyond recognition.

Marriage Guidance Counsellors give us many instances of couples arriving for their final reconciliatory meeting. The husband has disengaged himself from his mistress and on his wife's insistence has even sacked his secretary. But when they arrive it is perfectly clear that, although the wife may have overcome her drink problem, may in fact have been totally dry for the last one hundred days, she is at the moment a dishevelled glassy-eyed drunken slut with laddered stockings and one heel missing from her shoes.

Every day, all over the country, tens of thousands of people are personally begging other tens of thousands of people to 'please arrive sober, just this once, for this occasion at least', just for once in their lives to get through a particularly important assignment without getting plastered. The second group, fortunately, contains a high proportion of Asmolians endowed with involuntary breakout patterns and the result of the begging and pleading, the reasoning and the promising, will be, for the first group, irrevocable doom.

THE BENDER

Total loss of control over alcohol and time

Now this is indeed success in one of its most spectacular forms. For days, in some superb cases for weeks, the student is missing without trace. Without trace, that is, in the sense that no one can track him down, though everyone seems to know where he is. Dutiful wives inform his employers of his bad dose of heavy influenza; dutiful friends tell his wife that his car has broken down, that his mother is in hospital, that he's spending the weekend with colleagues or that he's been called to Shropshire on business. Acquaintances inform friends that he was last seen gambling heavily in Soho and club proprietors report that only three nights ago he was entertaining four women during an all-night session, at which fifty pounds worth of damage was done to the premises. Where is he? What's he doing? What has happened?

Well, there is one person who most certainly does not have the answers to these important questions. Having been forced on to the dry for weeks, perhaps months, the advanced Asmolian has broken out and is now experiencing a stupendous excess of release. And all the Asmolian factors are at work: he's lost his sense of time and does not know or care what day it is; his intake of alcohol is compulsive and massive, his memory has gone; and his personality has changed to that of a dictactor with no more worlds to conquer. Money, quite rightly, has become meaningless and inexhaustible; the myth of sexual morality, and indeed any other idiotic form of morality, has been washed away by a sea of cleansing chemicals; and our successful student is now free in a world devoid of such sordid and humanly unnatural restrictions as wives, jobs and Savings Accounts.

We know enough about the workings of society not to be surprised that everyone will be trying to put a stop to all this. Spouses, if they can find the joyous reveller, will try to reduce the partner to their own level of mundane monotony. Colleagues, unable to stand their own envy any longer, will pressure him to at least make an appearance at the office. Bank Managers, noting with hatred the establishments to which the cheques are made out, will stop payments. Relatives will side with whoever they're not related to and children will be coerced into a form of filial piety involving the denunciation of one or other parent.

None of these treacherous activities and traps will have the slightest effect on the Asmolian, provided he continues to pour in the essential juices. People seem to realise this instinctively, and have a vicious habit of making their frontal assault in the morning, long before the King of Misrule has had time to affect a cure. This is why it is essential to keep on the move; one night in an hotel, the next with a friend, followed by a short stay at the club; then disappear into another hotel.

In the end, however, those on the hunt will be forced to resort to the medical profession. At first it will be just the family doctor. If this does not bring him into line, they will have recourse to heavier guns. The only defence against this is to keep moving and keep scooping. After all, we are free – and they are not.

THE SCHIZOID SLIP

The substitution of one reality for another

The Schizoid Slip is at one and the same time the most important Asmolian clincher and the most difficult to explain to those who have not enjoyed it, in spite of the fact that it is, in its milder manifestations, the most common. This is so because it raises awkward questions of personal identity and the puzzling principles of reality.

Those of you who have studied philosophy, in particular the works of Descartes and Sartre, will know what I'm talking about. For those of you who haven't, I will paraphrase, with two questions, the major contributions of these philosophers to the history of intellectual endeavour:

'WHO AM I?'

and

'WHAT THE HELL IS GOING ON?'

For the Asmolian, the answers to these questions can be vitally important. Sitting, stupid, in the Chico Bar on 47th

Street, raising his glass again to the bartender, he could be anyone, anyone at all. And for himself, the person he is least likely to be is himself – which is confusing for a man waving an empty glass at a bartender.

As for what is going on about him – the C.I.A. are everywhere. The F.B.I., Scotland Yard, the Special Branch, the Fraud Squad, agents of the Sub-Committee on Un-American Activities, the Inland Revenue, the Ghost Squad, the Secret Service, the Royal Canadian Mounted Police and even linguistically disorientated murderers from Interpol – all these surround him. And all he is doing (whoever he may happen to be, or whoever he may happen to think he might possibly be) is trying to get a drink.

One of the most common occurrences of the Schizoid Slip reported to us usually takes place in a bar while the Asmolian is trying to cure himself. There you stand, alone, savagely hungover, trembling with your second vodka-tonic. At the other end of the bar a group of boys and girls seem to be enjoying themselves. It is while you are on your third drink that 'Asmolian Sensitivity' leads you to fully realise that the cause of their mirth and sudden outbreaks of laughter is *yourself*. Some bastard in that group is making jokes about you, smirking at your trembling hand, making merry mirth on your unshaven chops. In fact the longer you stare aggressively at them the easier it is to spot the trouble maker – it's that huge oaf whose father obviously has too much money, and probably his father before him.

Continuous unblinking glaring at them has no effect whatsoever: they are pretending they don't notice you. They are even acting as if they haven't seen you at all!

So you rest your fourth drink on the bar, straighten yourself up and walk smartly over to the bumptious buggers.

'Say that again!' you snarl at the second-generation ass.

'I'm sorry?' he queries in *mock innocence*.

'What you just said. You've been making jokes about me for the last half hour. Now just tell me what's so funny, you spunk bank account.'

'I'm so sorry, my dear chap, but we haven't been talking

about you at all. Actually, we've been telling rather dirty stories, if you must know. Nothing to do with you at all.'

It's at this point that you bop him on the nose. There's no sense playing along with his smart-ass pretence of not noticing you. Just give him another bash on the ear as he goes down.

Of course, during the court case, the press will refer to evidence of 'unprovoked assault in a public house.' But we know better: we know that an advanced Asmolian, during the clarity of a Schizoid Slip, has spotted one of the ignorant enemy and has dealt with him accordingly.

Other reports here at the Institute indicate to us that this phenomenon can quite often occur in heavy traffic, especially during rush-hour. You've been held up for so long that you're getting a bit jiggy yourself. You can't just abandon the car and dash into the nearest boozer, yet you're reluctant, right there in the middle of a crawling traffic jam, to reach for the glove compartment and start swigging it straight out of the bottle. It is then that you notice the Morris 1100 on your tail. It occurs to you that he has been around and about your car for some considerable time. And sure enough, at the next set of traffic lights the impudent bastard pulls up right along side of you. When you stare through the windows at him, he pretends to be looking straight ahead, unaware of your existence! Then, because you are looking at him and not at the traffic lights, he sneaks ahead and gets *in front of you!* And what does he do then? He just crawls along there in the middle of the road, defying you to overtake him. Through the benefit of a Schizoid Slip you have spotted the enemy trying to make a fool of you. Everytime you go to overtake him he pretends to be overtaking the car in front. When you get the chance you try to shoot through on the inside, only to have this tarmacadam torturer scare the hell out of you by wobbling dangerously near your bumper.

Well, at least you now *know* the reality of the situation and what is going on around you. Sooner or later, perhaps at the next set of traffic lights, you draw along side. You get out of your car and go over to his window, which you indicate he should roll down. Don't bother even talking to this son-of-a-bitch. As soon as the window is completely down, let him have it – right in the mush. After a stunned second or so, he will, nine times out of ten, look up at you – innocently! Never mind, you have by this time firmly grasped his door-frame with your left hand, and with this added leverage you let him have it again – right in the gob. As he can neither fall to the ground nor get out of the door, keep pumping away through the window until the bloodied head of the foolish temptor of fate is well and truly bowed. Now, open the door and notice how easily he rolls out on to the road, right in front of your feet. Though the traffic police are rushing towards you and several idiotic motorists have left their vehicles, kick his ear off. Even as the police are attempting to drag you away, you will still find it possible to stamp down on the evil-doer's face with crunching satisfaction.

If, at the trial, you enter a plea of Schizoid Slip as defence, you may find yourself sharing quarters with Bartholomew Kent, and with this in mind I should draw your attention to his letters which were dealt with in previous lectures.

As to the question of personal identity, this is a problem which has troubled some of the great minds throughout history: if I remember correctly Jesus Christ had some trouble with this one, and if God himself finds it a conundrum, it is hardly surprising that we mortals must turn to alcohol for help in the matter.

And it is here, and not in the Book of Revelations, that we find the answer. A good Schizoid Slip can provide certainty where before there was nagging, if unconscious, doubt. No, you are not the principal character in 'Death of a Salesman' – you're the boss! No, marriage is not an equal partnership, it is the domination of one personality by another – and you're on top, aren't you, fellah! And though, for a couple of days there, when you had no hootch, you appeared to be just a nobody – well, look now how that barman whips about as you shout at him; how people are roaring with laughter at your jokes and how cupidinous members of the opposite sex are eyeing with lascivious leers your every movement from the waist down.

Now it may well be that your present job doesn't fit in too well with this, your real self. So promote yourself a bit. In fact, while you're at it, promote yourself to the stature that you actually enjoy. Indeed, you'll probably find that your present firm isn't really worthy of you, so you had better change that too. And it might be as well to drop the odd clanger about the number of secretaries who had to leave for short trips abroad.

A good Schizoid Slip here, and you'll find your wife trying to tell you that you have a nine-to-five desk job and you'd better arrive there someday pretty soon. Well, there's no way of dealing with that kind of stupidity, so simply walk out of the door and join your new friends at the Executive Club.

*

These, then, are what we at the Institute consider to be the five most important indications of success. For those of you who are already enjoying them, they are self evident. For those of you who have not yet reached this stage, they can be reminders that success is always possible. So take heart when your closest friend turns aggressive towards you in drink. Even if he beats you about the place, remember that he is a confirmed Asmolian, and is thus superior to yourself. And if you find your husband's memory has become somewhat wobbly, that he has difficulty in remembering the story-line of the film he took you to yesterday, though wasn't really drunk until a great deal later – then wish him well, for he is one of us. If one of your colleagues, after setting out to be thoroughly sober at the Briefing Session, finds it impossible at the meeting to locate his own chair and in fact pukes on the Sales Analysis Chart, then you had better press on with further effort at your Asmolian course – for on the race to the top, he is ahead of you. As your friends go on ever-lengthening benders of debauchery, and even as some of them begin to realise that they are not in fact themselves, then take heart and renew your efforts.

Never despair – never! In weak moments, constantly bear in mind the axiomatic truth that success may be but one drink away.

Administration

Ladies and Gentlemen: Today will be my last talk to you in this present series of lectures, and I thought it might be a good idea if I gave you some impressions of the Institute itself and how it functions. Those of you who work at the Institute, or are at present patients here, may well feel that this will be somewhat tedious. I don't think so. No one person can say he knows the entire workings of any organisation, and in any case I intend to deal with this matter of Eamonn Kelly, a matter which the Press – and in particular that Bolshevik broadsheet of the Medical profession – has blown up out of all proportion.

I thought we might take a quick look at a typical day at the Institute, and then I might have time to go into some detail concerning a day which was quite *un*-typical – merciful Christ!

As most of you know, Miss Agatha Huntington awakes each patient at around 8.30 a.m. with a choice of three refreshing eye-openers – chilled orange juice, ice-cold Champagne, or both together.

Gawking commences almost immediately. There are few rules or regulations at the Institute, but it is understood by all patients that loitering in the lavatories, and thus creating a dangerous queue, is unpardonable. Also, each patient understands that if a mess is created during the rush, then whoever made the mess will damn well clean it up himself, or herself. In the event of there being more than one mess, or in fact a great deal of mess, then Looey and Bluey exercise their discretion as to who did what, and where. I can only assume that they are unfailingly just and correct in their decision, for no one seems too keen to dispute their findings.

On the dot of 9.30 a.m. the Cocktail Bar opens for cures. As it is very seldom nowadays that anyone is capable of pouring the first few drinks for themselves, Agatha acts as barmaid. (It will be appreciated, of course, that she necessarily started her cure some time before wakening the patients – if, indeed, she got to bed at all.) For some time now we have been experimenting with ways and methods of shortening the curing time. Our present system seems to be working out quite well, and we're cautiously optimistic that in the not too distant future we will have the curing-time cut to one hour exactly. At the moment everyone is doing all they can to achieve this figure, for they know that at any time after 10.30 a.m. Looey and Bluey are free to introduce the Chinese Bomb.

The Chinese Bomb treatment is a very simple therapy and has yet to fail in its purpose of separating those who are cured from those who are not. At any time after 10.30 a.m. the door to the Cocktail Bar bursts open. For a moment nothing happens: then the Bomb sails into the room and lands somewhere near the middle of the floor. Instead of a fuse, or in fact acting as a fuse, is a string of Chinese fire-crackers. This chain of banging doom can be varied by Looey and Bluey from three hundred right down to merely one explosion.

For grading purposes, those who, when the door crashes open, scream and drop their drinks are considered to be failing to the point of unco-operation and may well find themselves spending the afternoon in Ward D. Anyone rushing out the door runs into Looey and Bluey, who inflict immediate and instant therapy before hurling them back into the room – 'aiming' them, of course, to the very point of impending explosion. A grave black mark goes into the dossiers of those who, while staring with insane panic at the crackling fuse, break down and begin to weep.

After the explosion I myself enter the Bar and cast a professional diagnostic eye on the scene. Anyone discovered quietly pouring themselves another drink gets full marks, while those found even pretending to be carrying on with their conversation get a gold star. In the old days, of course, Hamilton Hamilton used to get a bonus gold star by being discovered quietly continuing his perusal of the leading article in *The Guardian.* (Some time ago, however, my growing suspicion that Hamy was weakening off and in fact reduced to only pretending to read the leading article was confirmed on the morning he broke down completely and was found to be eating the sports page.)

The next hour or so is given over to Group Therapy, after which time the pubs are open and the patients are encouraged to go down to the local, The Bells, and pay for their own drinks. And those of you who wonder why all patients are restricted to The Bells, and are actively discouraged from entering any other pub, should remember a certain patient, a Mr Joad, who, during a pretty firm Schizoid Slip, actually accused me of a rake-off from The Bells and spent the next fourteen days in Ward D.

As the pub is open for lunch, patients buy for themselves whatever they think will stay down. This quite often turns out to be an Ultra-Vitamin pill with gin and tonic.

During the afternoon, while the research team is engaged in experimental work, patients are free to do as they please. Some collapse back into their beds, though an increasingly large number of patients are finding that after a few hours of comatose gonking, a bad dose of the horrors can set in. Some stagger off to the local cinema; it doesn't matter that they've seen the same picture for almost a week. They always seem to drop off into drunken snoring at differing stages of the story and so are seldom bored by repetition – assuming that they can remember the plot-line at all. Others crowd frantically around the public call-box at the Institute and conduct matters of high finance: Turf Accountants and Stock Brokers are inundated with wagers and investments of an acutely bizarre nature.

The Cocktail Party starts at 7.30 in the evening. Agatha, if she's really up to it, acts as hostess. Usually, as with most of the patients, she is outrageously over-cured by this time and can be extremely witty and vivacious; though recently she has tended to sag from time to time, what with her long day, early rising and multitudinous duties – to say nothing of her hour-long 'therapeutic' sessions in Eamonn Kelly's room. On these occasions she tends to cry a good deal and it is usually necessary to fetch the zombie Kelly from his room and bring him to the bar. Then she will sit quietly in the corner with the Wise One, stroking his head and telling him children's stories.

The Dinner Party is at ten o'clock and by this time everyone, but *everyone*, is gargled out of their wits. The food (which has, with varying degrees of success or disaster, been cooked or burnt or simply defrosted by the female patients) is heaved on to the table or the floor by Looey and Bluey, who act as waiters. I, as host, sit at the head of the table, and carve the joint while making pleasantries with one and all. The wine is opened by Looey and served by Bluey, and no one really cares that sometimes Looey opens them by simply smashing the necks off against the wall, or that Bluey can be seen swigging openly from the bottle as he moves from guest to guest. Everyone is in tremendously good form and we are, if not one big happy family, then twenty or thirty big happy families.

Sometimes brawling breaks out at these parties, in which case Looey and Bluey invariably set about the innocent and injured parties and 'aim' them out into the night. Should the situation deteriorate to a general free-for-all then Looey and Bluey will, with a nod from me, mill about the room, smashing down all and sundry. When everyone, barring myself, has been beaten to their knees we all return to what's left of the table and start all over again.

After-dinner drinking takes place in the Cocktail Bar. Everyone crashes around behind the bar, serving themselves copiously with highly charged fuel. As they pass out, each patient is carted off to his or her or somebody else's bedroom. Agatha, if she's in good form, will start taking her clothes off, *all* her clothes off, much to the disinterest of all. Everyone will have undergone profound personality changes, and it is not entirely without entertainment that we watch those enjoying a Schizoid

Slip as they hunt about in the darkened grounds for members of the Flying Squad or representatives of the Press. Not only this – their activities keep visits from those agencies to a minimum.

Those who manage to drink their way right through the night get full marks; a gold star goes to those who, having drunk away the night, appear as usual in The Bells; and those who – though they may temporarily have to be restrained in Ward D – manager, by continuous sleepless drinking, to achieve startling insanity, get a bonus gold star.

This then, is more or less what takes place at the Institute on a normal day. Now, for those of you who do not know what took place on May 16th last, and for those hysterical hounds from the mass media who will not leave us alone over this question of Eamonn Kelly, I will try to describe to you a quite untypical day at the Institute.

*

The events leading up to those of May 16th actually had their origins in a conference held in my study on May 1st. We were all agreed that the time had come for our first experiment with a human subject, and we were clarifying exactly what this experiment should entail. I think I put it rather succintly to my staff:

'We've learnt a great deal about alcohol. Clinical tests have shown what it is, what it does and how dependence upon it can be induced. But we've been dealing with the *norm*, and those of you with scientific training will know full well that you can learn most about the normal by studying the abnormal. Therefore, our first human experiments should be with the abnormal.

'With this in mind, I'm going to suggest that one of us goes on a stupendous bender. The volunteer will be locked into his or her room, and for fourteen days will be given as much alcohol as he or she can consume. On the fourteenth day, all alcohol will cease and the subject will undergo rapid withdrawal.

'Now then, as I have to run this place it can't possibly be me. Do I have any volunteers?'

It was Agatha who spoke up immediately.

'Make it Eamonn Kelly, Professor. Oh, do! You've been restricting his drinking for weeks and weeks. He came here to drink and I think he deserves a decent break.'

'Of course I've had to reduce his drinking,' I replied. 'It's either that or Ward D. I mean to say, who the hell can stand Irish rebel songs twenty hours a day?'

'He sings ballad songs as well,' she retorted. 'His "Galway Bay" may be a trifle sentimental, but his "Wild Colonial Boy" can be quite stirring, and his rendition of "Boola Vogue" is positively inspiring.'

'Agatha, dear, that's *ridiculous!* He's terrible. Awful. And without wishing in any way to imply anything at all, I must warn you about relationships between staff and patients.'

'I'm only human,' she pronounced.

'But *he's* not, Agatha. That's the point. He's a joke. A stage Irishman, if ever there was one.'

'Well, he'll certainly drink more than any of us. And the fact that he'll enjoy it more should not influence your objective judgment, Professor.'

In the end, Agatha won the day. A secret peep-hole, with magnifying eye-glass, was screwed into Eamonn's door and he was duly informed of the experiment. I wish I could describe his ecstasy on hearing the news, but I'm afraid he was so excited that I could not understand him. 'Bejesus!' is an understandable, if meaningless, exclamation; no doubt 'Bedad!' means something to those who live in Eire, perhaps only Kerry; but I'm afraid I was utterly stumped when it came to 'Begob!'

The next two weeks were acoustically excruciating for all of us. As each new case of Irish Whiskey was taken to his room by Looey or Bluey, we all dreaded the results. As far as we could make out, the first three days were taken up with re-living the peasant uprising of 1798. As in all Irish politics the world over, the 'movement' was riddled with informers, traitors and those of devious ambition. After some initial successes, principally in the town of Wexford, the peasant army went on the piss and were efficiently and ruthlessly put down by the Militia. However, those who were present at the Institute last May will never 'fear to speak of '98':

Who fears to speak of '98,
Who cringes at the name?
When cowards take our Lord in vain,
Who blushes at the shame?

He's half a slave
Or all a knave
Who slights his country thus;
But you, Sir,
My good Sir,
Will fill your cup with us!

There are quite a few verses to this rebel rant, and we were to become very familiar with Wexford and Father Murphy. Kerry itself, of course, received due attention:

'Twas Kerry here and Kerry there,
'Twas Kerry, K-E-RRRR-Y everywhere,
And all across the midnight air,
There rang the war cry –
KERRY!

Few of us slept during this experiment. At odd times during the night there would come the defiant battle cry, 'Up the Rebels!' followed shortly by Eamonn crashing into something. At other times he would defend himself from the Black-and-Tans by hurling empty bottles at them or barricading the door with his bed, amid much scraping and screaming.

Mercifully, May 11th eventually arrived and from then on we were able to survive only by remembering that the end was near. I accompanied the last case of whiskey as it was carried to his room.

'Eamonn, this is your last case. You've been drinking something between three and four bottles a day, and this dozen will take you to the fourteenth day. After that you're on the dry, Eamonn.'

'FREE ALL POLITICAL PRISONERS!' he shouted at

me, then commenced to rip open the case.

On the morning of May 15th, Eamonn ran out of booze. The noise was terrible and the crying pitiful. He'd scream through the key-hole for a drink, then try to unhinge the door by beating and kicking it. Then he would collapse into a stupor, slobbering and weeping.

We watched all this through the tiny peep-hole with its wide-angle lens. It was a sickening sight, truly. Few of us could watch for very long, and we had to innovate a voluntary observation rota. Even Hamilton Hamilton, who was, at that time, still a strong man, asked to be relieved of this onerous duty. But I had to point out to him that the less he did, the more each one of us had to do. It is to his credit that he came into line, and even took over Agatha's turns at the peep-hole, for she seemed to be breaking up under the strain of this enforced voyeurism.

'For God's sake,' she moaned at me. 'Give the man a drink. He's dying in there.'

'The history of medical research and advance,' I informed her, 'is based on risk – and is epitomised by martyrdom.'

*

May 16th started quite normally. The Bar had been open for half an hour when the first indication of doom arose. Looey came into my study.

'A new patient has just arrived, Master. What do we do with him?'

'New patient?' I queried, for I was not expecting any. 'What's his name?'

'Dickson, Chief. Simon Dickson.'

'Well, well. Excellent. Send him in, will you?'

'He's on a stretcher, Captain.'

'What do you mean he's on a stretcher?' I asked rather loudly. 'How the hell did he get here on a stretcher?'

'Ambulance, Admiral.'

'Whose ambulance? What ambulance? Where did he come from? Oh, Christ, I suppose I'd better have a look.'

True enough, just inside the hall door there was an unconscious man on a stretcher. He was a tall, thin man in his early forties. His face had not been shaved for some time and his dark hair was matted. On his chest there lay an ominous envelope.

'Who brought him in here?' I asked as I opened the envelope.

'The ambulance men. We wasn't to know nothing, was we?'

On a plain piece of paper was written a short note which was to make it all clear.

Dear John,

As I explained on the telephone, we do not have a bed here for Mr Simon Dickson, and so I am sending him over to you for massive sedation. There will be a bed here for him in a day or so.

If, however, it proves necessary to keep him with you after he wakes up, I would suggest that he has no visitors. It would appear that he passed out while beating up his wife, and I feel that a visit from her or the police might prove disturbing.

Thank you again for your help.

Charles.

'They've sent him to the wrong place!' I exclaimed. 'This poor bugger's supposed to be in the bin.'

We all stared down as Mr Dickson attempted to move. His hands felt along the sides of the stretcher and his eyes eased open.

'Aaagh,' he said.

With woozey eyes he looked at each of us in turn, then glanced down at the stretcher.

'So I'm inside again,' he said, more or less to himself. 'What a bitch of a wife.'

'Mr Dickson, my name is Professor Asmol, and I shall be in charge of your treatment here. Now if you'd care to get up I'd like to take you along for medication.'

'The bloody pills,' he swore softly as he prised his long frame to an upright position. 'All right, lead the way. Let's get it over with.'

With Looey and Bluey on either side of him, I led the

fatalistic Mr Dickson into the Cocktail Bar.

'These are your fellow patients, Mr Dickson. You'll be getting to know them quite well in the coming days.'

But Dickson had slumped into a chair and could only respond with a slight wave of his hand. He seemed unable to re-open his eyes.

'I think, Agatha, that our Mr Dickson could do with a little something.'

Agatha reached for the gin bottle as Dickson spoke to me.

'What are you starting with?' he asked, his eyes still closed. 'Tuonal? Nembutal? A good jab of . . . Christ! Ice cubes!'

With this Dickson was out of his chair and holding my arm, staring wide-eyed at my forehead.

'Professor, I need help. I'm having delusions. I distinctly heard the sound of ice dropping into a glass. A heavy glass, probably crystal. I'd know that sound anywhere in the world and . . . Jesus! Now I can hear the glass being filled. This is a bad one, Professor. Next I'll be hearing the tonic being opened . . . Good Lord! There it is.'

Simon Dickson now stared about the room, his eyes finally resting on the gin and tonic which Agatha was proffering.

'Professor, you've got to help me. Help me! I think I'm in a bar and someone is offering me a gin and tonic. Christ, Professor, what has happened to my mind? I can see other people here as well, and *they all have drinks in their hands!* Oh, God, I've flipped completely.'

'Not at all, Mr Dickson,' I reassured him. 'You are in the Cocktail Lounge of the Asmolian Institute, and you are amongst friendly people who are having a drink. That is your's on the bar. I suggest you drink it. Perhaps then things will not appear so unreal.'

Dickson reached for his drink, but managed only to grab empty space.

'Aaagh,' he said, finally getting his paw on the tumbler. But it was obvious that he didn't stand a chance of getting it to his lips.

'Can I help you?' I asked, grasping his wildly shaking hand.

'Tea towel,' was all he replied. 'Just give me the tea towel.'

With trembling hands, Dickson folded the tea towel lengthwise, then draped it around his neck. With one end of the towel in his right hand he took a firm grip on the glass. With his left hand he pulled downwards on the towel, thus producing a pulley action which slowly brought the rattling glass to his face. Obviously knowing that it would be risky to lower the glass, he finished off the drink at one go. Then he returned the glass to the bar, addressing himself to the gin as he did so:

'Now stay down, you bastard. Just stay there.'

At 10.35 a.m., as Mr Dickson (feeling somewhat better with his third drink in his hand) was beginning to comprehend what was happening, the door crashed open.

'Aaaaagh!' he screamed, throwing his drink all over the ceiling.

'No, no, not this time,' I called out, but it was too late. The Chinese Bomb flew into the room and landed in the middle of the floor.

'Aaaaagh!' Dickson screamed as he scrambled madly on to the bar. Aaaaaaaaaaaaaaaaagh!'

When the explosion came, Mr Dickson collapsed backwards, full length behind the bar. It took us an entire hour to straighten him out, but even then he kept a watchful eye on the door as he attempted to re-cure himself.

*

The next intimation of disaster came at noon.

'Get up, Professor,' said Hamilton Hamilton.

This was, for me, confusing. I was under the impression that I had stayed for an hour or so in the Cocktail Lounge, joining Dickson in his magnificent cure. Then I had returned to my office and was now gazing thoughtfully out of the window.

'Will you for Christ's sake come out from under that desk!' Hamilton was telling me sternly.

'Nonsense,' I replied, realising now that Ham did have a much firmer grip on reality than myself. As I crawled back on to my chair I explained: 'This whole question of balance will have to be looked into. I was just experimenting there with the sensations of horizontal . . .'

'You're corned, Professor. You're stewed up to the ears.'

'Don't be insulting, Ham. Might I remind you of the existence of Ward D.'

'That's just it, Professor. And in any case I'm not insulting you. We all like to see you practicing what you preach. The trouble is that there is someone here to see you. A Dr Wilson.'

'Throw him out,' I answered with instant decision. 'Where's Looey and Bluey?'

'Fortunately, *they* haven't found him. Listen, Professor. Try to hear what I'm telling you. It's *Inspector* Wilson, from the Ministry of Health. And he just happens to be a doctor. Now remember Ward D, Professor? It was your brilliant idea to send all the bills for the swimming pool for payment to the Ministry. Now this Inspector is here to check up.'

'Well, why didn't the fool make an appointment?'

'He probably did,' Hamilton sighed. 'Just look at the unopened letters on your desk.'

'Well, what the hell's Agatha up to? She's supposed to be responsible for secretarial work around here. Running this place is no easy task, Hamilton.'

'Agatha's overworked as it is, Professor. And quite frankly, though the last two weeks with Eamonn have been hell for all of us, she really has taken it badly. And in any case, this doesn't solve the problem of Inspector Wilson.'

'No, it doesn't, does it? Christ, what I am I to do? Hamilton, rush and get me a drink. Then slowly – leaving me time to lower it – bring Dr Wilson here.'

I had managed to get the drink down, and was secreting the glass in my drawer when Hamilton brought in the Inspector. This bureaucratic spy was nearing retirement, wore rimless spectacles, and obviously had not laughed for a generation.

'Professor Asmol,' he wheezed as Hamilton left the room. 'I am Doctor Wilson from the Ministry. Sorry I'm a bit late, but as I explained in my letter, I'm not familiar with this part of the world. And you certainly are tucked away here, aren't you?'

'Deliberately so, Doctor,' I answered authoritatively as I waved him to a chair. 'Quite deliberate. We feel that our patients should enjoy privacy, and, in a sense, isolation, while undergoing treatment.'

'I was under the impression that this was a research institute,' he said evilly.

'And so it is, Doctor,' I replied firmly, my mind racing for answers to this member of the medical Gestapo. 'But along with the staff and students, we also have patients here under observation.'

'Normal treatment, I suppose?'

'Not absolutely, Doctor. No. Not in the strictest sense of the word. But then what *is* normal these days? And we've discovered some pretty unusual approaches to the problem, as you may know. I intend to deal with all these matters in my lectures at the end of the year.'

'Yes, of course, Professor,' he smiled his small white porcelain teeth at me. 'No wish to pry into your work here. My main task is simply to verify to my department that you do exist – you'd be surprised at the amount of fraudulent activity going on these days – and that this construction, "Ward D", has in fact been completed.'

'A pleasure, Doctor, a pleasure,' I stated uselessly.

'This appears to be an *underground* construction,' he said with something like distaste. 'Rather odd, isn't it?'

'Not at all, no, not at all,' and my mind staggered for words. 'Planning permission is almost impossible around here. In any case, though Ward D is in no way punative – we don't agree with such an approach – we thought it would be most depressing for the patients to be constantly aware of any sort of Block House, or Detention Centre. We have to fight depression here. We needed something near to hand, yet quite inconspicuous.'

'But the bills, Professor. They all seem to come from the Harrow Pool and Sauna Co. Ltd.'

'Well, they're experts in the field, don't you know? And they did give us the lowest quote.'

'But it appears you applied to have a special water supply arranged.'

'Really?' I lied outright. 'First I've heard of it.'

'Well, we know of a rejection to such an application.'

'No doubt those people at Harrow Pool and Sauna apply automatically once they start to dig a hole.'

'Well, it's rather odd, but I don't suppose it matters. As long as you're satisfied with the work, Professor.'

'Oh, but completely. Excellent people. First class job in every way.'

'Good,' this Civil Service spy nodded. 'Now if I could just have a quick look at the Institute – without interrupting you, of course – then an inspection of Ward D. And I'll be on my way.'

And so I took this walking paper clip to see the cubicles and some of the patients' rooms. Throughout this he was asking damnably embarrassing questions. One of them was downright insulting, and he was quite outright with it:

'Have you been drinking, Professor?' he asked bluntly.

'Good Lord, no!' I exclaimed. 'Never touch the stuff. Hardly do to have the staff, to say nothing of the head of the Institute, even tasting a drop of alcohol.'

'But you smell of it, Professor. Positively reek of the stuff. Whisky, I should imagine.'

'Oh, that,' I gestured meaninglessly. 'Accident in the Lab. this morning. Damned nearly drowned in the stuff. Haven't had time to change yet.'

'But then why are you staggering, Professor?'

'The burden of work,' I answered nobly. 'You've no idea the pressure I've been under these last two weeks.'

I was, at this point, trying to ease him past the Cocktail Lounge from which, unfortunately, there came the constant sounds of yelling and uproarious luaghter.

'What's in here?' he asked, turning smartly on his heels.

Before I could stop him the horrible man was through the door. Immediately Dickson, crazed with booze, was all over him.

'Aaagh, what you in here for, little old man? I beat up my

wife, that's what I did. She's a slut, you know. An absolute slut!'

'Good heavens,' mouthed the dirty little doctor. 'This is a bar!'

'Yes, indeed, Doctor Wilson,' I tried to explain. 'We don't expect our patients to go out into the world of temptation without first *overcoming* their problem in simulated circumstances.'

'I'm sorry, Professor,' Agatha said to me. 'I know they should be at The Bells, but Simon has been amusing us so with stories of his wife . . .'

'The Bells?' Wilson queried with an incredulous sneer. 'But that's a pub. I passed it on my way here.'

'Some of our advanced patients,' I rushed to explain, 'have progressed to the point where they are encouraged to enter public houses and exercise *control.* That's the secret of our success, Doctor. *Overcome* the problem, then exercise *control.*'

'Success?' he blurted. 'Success? But everyone in this room is totally drunk . . .'

Crack-BOOM!

The explosion seemed to rock the building. All conversation immediately ceased and we stood in silence, the echo still in our ears. It was the damnable doctor who immediately came to the correct interpretation:

'That was a gun shot!'

'Nonsense,' I laughed. 'The boiler. It's been giving us some trouble lately. In fact we may have to apply . . .'

'Professor Asmol,' Wilson told me. 'I was a Medic at Normandy. I'd know that sound . . .'

Crack-BOOM! Crack-BOOM!'

There could be no doubt now. We found ourselves rushing along the corridor to Eamonn Kelly's room. But Hamilton was already there, peering through the peep-hole. I pushed him to one side and had a look for myself.

Eamonn was sitting on the floor, his back to the wall. Across the room, lined up against the wall, were the empty bottles from his last case of Irish Whiskey. In his two hands he held the largest and ugliest looking pistol I have ever seen. I stood back, aghast.

'What do you make of it, Hamilton?'

Hamilton raised his ear from the key-hole and replied with what was, for him, considerable astonishment.

'It's some form of court-martial. The empty bottles, it appears, are on trial for desertion.'

'But the gun?' I asked in true amazement. 'What about that terrible cannon?'

'That,' Wilson told us as he stepped back from the peep-hole, 'is a Parabellum. An extremely heavy, large bore gun, quite popular at the time of the Easter Rising in Ireland in 1916. Tell me, Professor,' he continued, 'do many of your patients carry side-arms?'

'Oh, shut up,' I snorted. 'We have an emergency. Looey!' I called, 'and you, Bluey. Disarm that man before he does himself a serious injury.'

The door was opened by Hamilton. Looey and Bluey walked purposefully into the room. But Eamonn simply turned, shouted something about the Mayor of Limerick and fired. A large section of plaster came away from the wall beside me – but not before Looey and Bluey were out of the room.

'Not us, Guv. We wasn't paid for no shooting. Give us a couple of grenades and we'll get him for you. Otherwise *you* can walk in there and get your balls blown off.'

I could only agree with the realism expressed here. In an attempt to learn more about what was going on inside the room I put my ear to the key-hole.

'You weren't *there*,' Eamonn accused one of the remaining bottles. 'This court is not interested in armaments. Sure, weren't half the men without guns, and didn't they pick up their pikes and run the enemy through. But you weren't even there. This court finds you guilty of desertion and sentences you to be shot.'

Almost immediately there was a terrible Crack-BOOM! followed by the showering of glass about the room.

'Professor Asmol,' Wilson announced in the voice of officialdom. 'Ever since I've arrived here I've had the distinct feeling that not all is as it should be. It will be my duty to report that this Institution is not only a fraud, but also a positive risk to the community. Your patients are drunk, your staff are drunk, and even you yourself seem to be suffering badly from acute alcoholic poisoning. On top of all this, at least one of your patients – or is he staff, God knows what the difference might be – is free to indulge in gunplay, shooting at empty liquor bottles. Bottles, furthermore, which he has obviously just consumed, to judge by his state of complete mental derangement.'

'Now you've done it, Wilson,' I sneered. 'I was prepared to put up with the usual Ministry farce, knowing that our work is not yet acceptable to fools like you. But now you've gone too far. So you came to see Ward D, did you? Well, see it you most certainly shall. Looey! Bluey! Throw this medical moron into Ward D – for LIFE!'

The last that was seen of Dr Wilson was his pitiful frame being 'aimed' at terrible velocity along the corridor. Pleased with this sight, I returned my ear to the key-hole.

'No, sir, you were not at the G.P.O. You were not at the Customs House. And Cathal Brugha tells me you weren't with him. Then where were you? Informing, that's what you were at. Informing! You're guilty, and the sentence of this court is that you be shot.'

Crack-BOOM! Crack-BOOM! Crack-BOOM!

'God,' I trembled. 'We must put a stop to this.'

'Let me go in,' Agatha suggested immediately. 'He wouldn't possibly hurt me. I mean to say, he wouldn't *shoot* me, Professor. And I'm sure I could talk him out of it. Please, Professor?'

'You might have a point there, Agatha. If only I could be sure he'd recognise you. He is completely deranged, you know. If he thinks empty bottles are deserters from various Irish uprisings, what will he think of something that moves about on two legs?'

'He'll know it's me, Professor. At least let me have a try.'

'As you wish, Agatha. But do have a care.'

With this, Hamilton opened the door and Agatha walked slowly into the room.

'Hello, Eamonn. It's me, Agatha. I've come to see if . . .'

'You Saxon slut!' shouted Eamonn and immediately grabbed her by the arm, hurling her across the room and on to the bed. He then set about tearing off her clothes.

'We'd better go in,' Hamilton announced bravely.

'Do you really think so?' I queried sagaciously. 'No harm done, really. We can always buy dear Agatha some new knickers.'

However, a further glance through the peep-hole showed that Eamonn had put the monstrous gun on his bed-side table and was inflicting upon Agatha the indignities of complete rape.

'Time to go in,' Hamilton announced, reaching for the door handle.

'Now, Ham,' I cautioned. 'There is nothing we can do now about Agatha's virginity. And as I say, we can buy her heaps and heaps of new knickers. But at least the bugger's not shooting anyone.'

My sagacity was to no avail. Hamilton opened the door and we marched in. We at once put our hands very high in the air as, without any break in the rhythmic crime, the hideous gun was pointed at us, indicating that we should back out of the room. This we did, slowly and carefully.

'Well, that's it,' I said as Hamilton closed the door behind us. 'It's a question of armed rape, and there's damn all we can do about it.'

'You didn't notice?' Hamilton asked as we turned into the corridor, heading, with resignation, towards the Cocktail Bar.

'Notice?' I asked. 'Notice what?'

'It was Agatha who was pointing the gun.'

*

Of course, the rest of the day was a shambles. No food was produced; Agatha made no appearance at all – I simply found the gun on my desk next morning; organisation faltered badly and no one made any attempt to leave the Cocktail Lounge.

Agatha never discusses Eamonn. She simply leaves us for about an hour in the morning for what she refers to as 'therapy'. There's no sense in trying to look through the peep-hole: once she is inside the room she simply covers this with a piece of plaster. I did, during one such 'therapy', try to listen through the key-hole, but the conversation seemed unintelligible.

'Hello, Eamonn. It's me, Agatha. I've come to see you.'

'Ah, me sweet colleen. I've got something for you.' Look at this!'

'Oh Eamonn! I say, you really are a good boy today.'

Sometimes, in the afternoon, I go in to see Eamonn and have a chat with him. He is always amiable, confabulating away like a computer with a vivid imagination.

'Hello, Eamonn. Having a nice day?'

'To be sure, Professor. Went for a walk with Agatha this morning. Then we went to The Bells for lunch. Went to the pictures, too.'

Eamonn, of course, has never left his room. But ask him what he had for lunch and we will almost drool over the memory of his pork pie. Ask him what the film was about, and he will give you the next episode in The Decline and Fall of The Irish Free State. But no matter what he confabulates, no matter what pleasures his non-existent memory may provide him with, there is always: 'Went for a walk with Agatha this morning.'

And now, I think, I have given you a pretty good picture of 'Administration' at the Asmolian Institute.

*

This brings us to the end of this present series of lectures. And I do wish, Ladies and Gentlemen, that I could leave you with some idea or stirring suggestion which has not already occurred to me. But as far as I am aware I have conveyed to you, within the references initially laid down, all the information and ideas I set out to explain.

Instead, I would like to address a few remarks to those not present, to those who will be reading these lectures in book form and among whom there will necessarily number a substantial percentage of successful and failed, conscious or unconscious, Asmolians. Also among this group will figure an even higher percentage of people personally and directly involved with a student of Asmolianism – even perhaps some freak failure. For our social surveys have shown that for every Asmolian there are six or seven people whose lives – dependently, emotionally or financially – are radically involved.

We know that no man is an island: our present society is comprised of groups. No man can be run down by a bus and remain an isolated incident; wife, mother, dependent children, colleagues, employer, contractual obligations, insurers, promoters, emulators, personal friends and the bus driver – all are directly involved, some more accountably than others.

It is the same with all accidents or diseases which can be either temporarily or permanently crippling – or both, depending to such an extent (as just mentioned)on those directly involved along with the victim. Disease and lightning are no longer selective: we deal in social diseases and sheet lightning. Disaster is communal – and there are more visitors to the Terminal Ward than there are cadavers.

And failure itself, like success, can never be permanent. Both, by their nature, must be repeated – or they reverse themselves. With this in mind let me pass on to you the words carefully written down for me by a man who had struggled for a long time with the problems of God and self-destruction.

> *It is immaterial to know whether there is a God or not: hope is a human virtue and it is a virtue to be forcibly squeezed from the soft but indestructable marrow of our despairing souls.*

THE END

HELLO SAILOR

by Petra Christian

A sexual drama on the high seas on board the *HMS Thruster*!

Sally Deenes is delighted to find that she has been adopted as ship's mascot by the crew of *HMS Thruster*. Jobless and penniless, she goes to Portsmouth to meet her new fans. The sailors are a friendly crowd and Sally soon makes herself at home – so comfortable that the ship sails with her still on board. It is not long before Sally and the jolly tars are engaged in exciting and dangerous manoeuvres at sea . . .

On sale at newsagents and booksellers everywhere.

RICH MAN, POOR MAN

by Irwin Shaw

From the author of THE YOUNG LIONS and TWO WEEKS IN ANOTHER TOWN comes the greatest novel to appear in post-war America. Truly global in the scope of its humanity and passion, RICH MAN, POOR MAN is the story of a generation at war with the values of its past, the hypocrisy and tension of its present and the terrifying inevitability of a shipwrecked future.

Rudolph is the romantic, who learns to live with doubt and make a fortune at 30. His brother Tom is the brute, whose acid-scarred American dream is coloured with boiling blood. Their sister, Gretchen, seduced by the small town's leading citizen, is the beauty in urgent search of a man – the only man – who can save her from herself.

'By the end of it we know America from coast to coast.'
— Daily Telegraph

NEW ENGLISH LIBRARY